Carl Dahlhaus

The Idea of Absolute Music

Translated by Roger Lustig

The University of Chicago Press · Chicago and London

Originally published as *Die Idee der absoluten Musik*, © 1978 Bärenreiter-
Verlag, Kassel.
The University of Chicago Press, Chicago 60637
The University of Chicago Press, Ltd., London
© 1989 by The University of Chicago
All rights reserved. Published 1989
Paperback edition 1991
Printed in the United States of America
98 97 96 95   543

Library of Congress Cataloging-in-Publication Data

Dahlhaus, Carl, 1928-
  [Idee der absoluten Musik. English]
  The idea of absolute music/Carl Dahlhaus; translated by Roger
    Lustig. p. cm.
  Translation of: Die Idee der absoluten Musik.
  Bibliography: p.
  Includes index.

  ISBN 0-226-13487-3 (paperback)
  1. Music—Philosophy and aesthetics. 2. Music—19th century—
History and criticism. I. Title.
ML3854.D3413 1989
781.1′7—dc20   89-4829

⊗ The paper used in this publication meets the minimum requirements of the
American National Standard for Information Sciences—Permanence of
Paper for Printed Library Materials, ANSI Z39.48-1984.

Contents

Translator's Introduction

In our century, the idea of absolute music has come to dominate musical life as never before. Our ritualized behavior and expectations at concerts reflect the worshipful attitude the last century developed toward music; musical analysis is only now becoming aware of even the structural functions of poetic meter; and the common assumption that librettos, plot summaries, programs, song lyrics, and so on somehow sully the "pure" experience of a work of musical art is a crude, extreme form of a dominant, and not necessarily conscious, attitude.

The idea of absolute music has many facets: the supremacy of music above other arts; the belief that words, instead of being an essential component of a piece of music, are either irrelevant to or even distracting from its meaning; the quasi-religious function of listening, whereby proper hearing of sublime music can afford the listener a glimpse of the infinite, or of the Beyond, or at least produce an esthetic experience above mundane ideas, images, and things; and the formalist view of music that equates form and content—that, as Adam Smith put it, the subject of a piece of music is within itself, i.e., the musical theme is the subject, whereas the subject of a painting, poem, or novel is outside the work itself.

Carl Dahlhaus has not only traced the prehistory, creation, and evolution of this complex of ideas; he has related it to more general trends in philosophy and to the specific works that stimulated its growth. The most striking philosophical construct he identifies is a hermeneutical model based on chains of opposites, which underlies most of the great esthetic debates of the seventeenth and eighteenth centuries. E. T. A. Hoffmann, writing about Beethoven's Fifth Symphony, used this model for the first full expression of the idea of sublime, exalted absolute music, its content and effect centered in its form rather than in a poetic or programmatic text. The Hegelian nineteenth century attempted to synthesize musical opposites: Nietzsche identified Wagner's music as a new synthesis of the Appolonian and Dionysian aspects; Halm saw Bruckner as having brought together the accomplishments of Bach and Beethoven in a new "culture" of music. Wagner himself, who actually (and disparagingly) coined the term "absolute music," accepted its premise as underlying even his own works, once he had recast his esthetic along Schopenhauer's lines.

The Idea of Absolute Music may be appearing at an opportune time. We are currently concerned with the idea of a canon—a body of art, literature, or philosophy that forms a core for the entire field, and that controls the ideas and assumptions used in study and criticism. Extremists on one side would have us accept the canon as it is or (really or ideally) was, and consider the issue of a canon to be irrelevant. Some on the other side, with a specific didactic or political purpose, would storm the ramparts that any canon represents, and constantly renew and reformulate it; but they do not necessarily examine the history of a canon, or the evolution of its purpose. In between, the debate rages about canons and their nature.

The musical canon is a special case. It has a very recent origin, less than two centuries ago; and we can easily identify the very events by which it was formed. Efforts on behalf of Beethoven's music in the 1830s and 1840s led to the modern, overtly historical concert that is the norm today; later, Bach was added as a second focus. The nineteenth century's new historical awareness in music affected everything that followed: new works were compared to the same few canonical ones, historicism in composition became more manifest, and progress replaced mere novelty as the yardstick of a new work. (Could Wagner have called his work "music of the future" had he not felt the burden of the recent past?)

The tension between progress and "classic" status finally grew unbearable. Charles Rosen traces the fragmentation of music after 1900 to a rupture in the composer's esthetic: one could no longer progress and at the same time hold one's work up to the standard of an ever-receding past. Much of the music of our century has openly confronted the canon; the growing use of quotation and recomposition, from Schoenberg, Berg, and Stravinsky to Berio, Crumb, and Kagel is but one form of this confrontation. At the same time, composers have strived to break entirely with the canon and its traditions on many levels, from Debussy's new ideas of structure, to serial techniques, to deliberate flouting by Satie, Cage, Stockhausen, and others of usual definitions of music.

We are aware of our musical canon, its genesis, and its relationship to current musical life. But the ideas behind it are not generally understood; and the central idea would seem to be that of absolute music. Professor Dahlhaus has tied the formation of the canon to the romantic esthetics of Wackenroder and Hoffmann, to Hegel's and Schopenhauer's philosophies, and to the centuries-old musical debates that the nineteenth century transformed. This broad analysis can show us what the canon actually represented to those who created it, and what it can mean to us. Perhaps, having understood this relatively new yet pervasive canon, we may proceed to a new understanding of others.

The Idea of Absolute Music is partly a sequel to, partly an expansion on, some themes from Dahlhaus's *Esthetics of*

Music, trans. William W. Austin (Cambridge, 1980). I have retained Austin's spelling of "esthetics"; if only his easy mastery of Dahlhaus's always-correct but always-difficult style came with it! Any success I have had is shared by Robert P. Morgan, Keith Falconer, and Juliet Beier, who offered improvements and encouragements whenever they were needed.

Carl Dahlhaus died on March 13, 1989, at the age of sixty, while this book was in preparation. For many years, he astounded the musicological world with the depth, breadth, quality, and sheer volume of his output. He accomplished this while battling the chronic ailments that finally led to his death.

His works on esthetics, musical historiography, Wagner, Schoenberg, the rise of tonality, the nineteenth century as a whole and in any number of individual aspects, and a dozen other topics are his monument. His seemingly effortless ability to synthesize seemingly disparate ideas and formulate the new understanding of history these ideas produce will be missed.

Roger Lustig

1
Absolute Music as an Esthetic Paradigm

The esthetics of music is not popular. Musicians suspect it of being abstract talk far removed from musical reality; the musical public fears philosophical reflections of the kind one ought to leave to the initiated, rather than plaguing one's own mind with unnecessary philosophical difficulties. Understandable as this mistrustful irritation with the sundry chatter of self-proclaimed music esthetics might be, it would be erroneous to imagine that esthetic problems in music are located in the hazy distance beyond everyday musical matters. In fact, when viewed dispassionately, they are thoroughly tangible and immediate.

Anyone who finds it burdensome to have to read the literary program of a symphonic poem by Franz Liszt or Richard Strauss before a concert; who asks for dimmed lights at a lieder recital, making the lyrics printed in the program illegible; who finds it superfluous to familiarize himself with the plot summary before attending an opera sung in Italian — in other words, whoever treats the verbal component of the music at a concert or opera with casual disdain is making a music-esthetic decision. He may consider his decision to be based on his own taste, when in fact it is the expression of a general, dominant tendency that has spread ever further in the last 150 years without sufficient recognition of its importance to musical culture. Above and beyond the individual and his coincidental preferences, nothing less than a profound change in the very concept of music is taking place: no mere style change among forms and techniques, but a fundamental transformation of what music is, what it means, and how it is understood.

Listeners who react in the manner described above are aligning themselves to a music-esthetic "paradigm" (to use the term that Thomas Kuhn applied to the history of science): that of "absolute music." Paradigms, basic concepts that guide musical perception and musical thought, form one of the central themes of one kind of music esthetics that does not lose itself in speculation, but instead explains assumptions that stand inconspicuously and little considered behind everyday musical custom.

Hanns Eisler, who made a serious attempt to apply Marxism to music and music esthetics, described the concept of absolute music as a figment of the "bourgeois period": an era he looked down on, but to which he also considered himself an heir. "Concert music, along with its social form, the concert, represents a historical epoch in the evolution of music. Its specific development is intertwined with the rise of modern bourgeois society. The predominance of music without words, popularly called 'absolute music,' the division between music and work, between serious and light music, between professionals and dilettantes, is typical of music in capitalist society."[1] However vague the term "modern bourgeois society" might be, Eisler seems to have felt certain that "absolute music" was not simply a "timeless" synonym for textless, independent instrumental music not bound to "extramusical" functions or programs. Instead, the term denoted a concept around which a specific historical epoch grouped its ideas concerning the nature of music. Eisler, surprisingly enough, calls the expression "absolute music" a "popular" one; this is doubtless hidden rancor against a coinage whose lofty claim—the connotation of absolute music allowing a premonition of the absolute—could hardly have escaped the son of a philosopher.

In the central European musical culture of the nineteenth century—as opposed to the Italian-French opera culture of the time—the concept of absolute music was so deep-rooted that, as we shall see, even Richard Wagner, though he polemicized against it on the surface, was convinced of its fundamental validity. In fact, it would hardly be an exaggeration to claim that the concept of absolute music was the leading idea of the classical and romantic era in music esthetics. As as we have already suggested, the principle was surely restricted geographically, but it would be premature at the very least to call it a provincialism, given the esthetic significance of autonomous instrumental music in the late eighteenth and early nineteenth centuries. On the other hand, the omnipresence of absolute music in the twentieth century must not be allowed to obscure the historical fact that—according to sociological, not esthetic, criteria—symphony and chamber music in the nineteenth century represented mere enclaves in a "serious" musical culture characterized by opera, romance, virtuoso display, and salon pieces (not to mention the lower depths of "trivial music").

That the concept of absolute music originated in German romanticism (despite the importance of its meaning within a music-historical context in the nineteenth century, a meaning that has taken on external, sociohistorical importance in the twentieth century), that it owed its pathos—the association of music "detached" from text, program, or function with the expression or notion of the absolute—to German poetry and philosophy around 1800, was clearly recognized in France, oddly enough, as an 1895 essay by Jules Combarieu shows. He writes that it was through "the German fugues and symphonies" that "thinking in music, thinking with sounds, the way a writer thinks with words" first entered the French consciousness, which had always clung to the connection between music and language to derive a "meaning" from music.[2]

Thus, despite its fundamental esthetic importance due to

3

the the artistic caliber and historical influence of the works that realized it, the geographical and social range of the idea of absolute music was quite limited at first. Likewise, the historical description in Eisler's rough sketch is too broad rather than too constricted. One can hardly speak of a music-esthetic paradigm for the "entire" bourgeois period. The idea of absolute music, which has a social character that cannot be reduced to any simple formula, stands in direct opposition to the music esthetics original to the "modern bourgeois society" of eighteenth-century Germany. Johann Georg Sulzer, in the article on "Music" in his *General Theory of the Fine Arts*, bases his verdict about autonomous instrumental music on moral philosophy—i.e., on the eighteenth century's authentically bourgeois mode of thought. His bluntness forms a curious contrast to Burney's generous term "innocent luxury"; this may be explained by the moral fervor of an upwardly mobile bourgeoisie as opposed to the laxity of an established one. Sulzer writes: "In the last position we place the application of music to concerts, which are presented merely as entertainments, and perhaps for practice in playing. To this category belong concertos, symphonies, sonatas, and solos, which generally present a lively and not unpleasant noise, or a civil and entertaining chatter, but not one that engages the heart."[3] The bourgeois moral philosopher's animus toward the musical diversions he found arcane and idle is unmistakable. If Haydn, in contrast, attempted to represent "moral characters" in his symphonies, as Georg August Griesinger reports,[4] then this esthetic intention meant nothing less than a vindication of the symphony's honor in an age whose bourgeoisie viewed art as a means of discourse about problems of morality, i.e., the social coexistence of human beings. Insofar as art withdrew from its purpose, it was scorned as a superfluous game of suspicious character, either above or below the bourgeoisie. This view applied primarily to literature, but, in a secondary sense, to music as well.

Only in opposition to the esthetic, of bourgeois origin and generated by moral philosophy, that Sulzer represented, was a philosophy of art formed that proceeded from the concept of the self-sufficient, autonomous work. In essays written between 1785 and 1788, Karl Philipp Moritz (whose ideas were accepted unreservedly by Goethe, hesitantly by Schiller) proclaimed the principle of *l'art pour l'art* with a bluntness attributable to his disgust with moral philosophy's rationalizations about art, and to the urge to escape into esthetic contemplation from the world of bourgeois work and life that he found oppressive. "The merely useful object is thus not something whole or perfect in itself, but attains that state only in fulfilling its purpose through me, or being completed within me. In observing the beautiful, however, I return the purpose from myself to the object: I observe the object as something not within me, but perfect in itself; that is, it constitutes a whole in itself, and gives me pleasure for the sake of itself, in that I do not so much impart to the beautiful object a relationship to myself, but rather impart to myself a relationship to it."[5] However, not only the Horatian *prodesse* but also *delectare*[6] is judged foreign to art; the recognition art demands, not the pleasure it provides, is decisive. "We do not need the beautiful in order that we may be delighted by it, as much as the beautiful requires us so that it may be recognized."[7] The one attitude that Moritz finds appropriate to the work of art is that of aesthetic contemplation in which self and world are forgotten; his fervor in describing it betrays his pietistic origins. "As long as the beautiful draws our attention completely to itself, it shifts it away from ourselves for a while, and makes us seem to lose ourselves in the beautiful object; just this losing, this forgetting of the self, is the highest degree of the pure and unselfish pleasure that beauty grants us. At that moment we give up our individual, limited existence in favor of a kind of higher existence."[8]

When the idea of esthetic autonomy, formerly limited to

the general artistic theory that applied primarily to poetry, painting, or sculpture, was extended to musical culture, it found an adequate expression in the "absolute" music that was disassociated from "extramusical" functions and programs. Though this seems natural and almost self-evident in hindsight, it was rather surprising at the time. As Jean-Jacques Rousseau's invective and Sulzer's contemptuous comments show, bourgeois thought held instrumental music without purpose, concrete concept, or object to be insignificant and empty—despite the Mannheim orchestra's success in Paris and Haydn's growing fame. Furthermore, the beginnings of a theory of instrumental music were distinguished by apologetics trapped in the opposition's terminology. When in 1739 Johann Mattheson characterized "instrumental music" as "sound oratory or tone speech," he was attempting to justify it by arguing that instrumental music is essentially the same as vocal music.[9] It too should—and can—move the heart, or usefully engage the listener's imagination by being an image of a comprehensible discourse. "In that case, it is a pleasure, and one needs much more skill and a stronger imagination to succeed without words than with their aid."[10]

Such early defenses of instrumental music, dependent on the model of vocal music, were based on the formulas and arguments of the doctrine of affections and the esthetics of sentiment.[11] As we shall show in a later chapter, when an independent theory of instrumental music developed, there was a tendency to contradict the sentimental characterization of music as the "language of the heart," or at least to reinterpret the tangible affects as ephemeral, abstract feelings divorced from the world. Novalis and Friedrich Schlegel combined this tendency with an aristocratic attitude of polemical irritation with the eighteenth-century culture of sentiment and social life, a culture they found narrow-minded. Like the moral-philosophical theory of art to which it was closely connected, the sentimental esthetic was truly of the bourgeoisie; it was only in contradiction to that esthetic, its social character, and the doctrine of utility that the principle of autonomy originated. Now instrumental music, previously viewed as a deficient form of vocal music, a mere shadow of the real thing, was exalted as a music-esthetic paradigm in the name of autonomy—made into the epitome of music, its essence. The lack of a concept or a concrete topic, hitherto seen as a deficiency of instrumental music, was now deemed an advantage.

One may without exaggeration call this a music-esthestic "paradigm shift," a reversal of esthetic premises. A bourgeois gentleman like Sulzer must have thought the elevation of instrumental music above and beyond any moral valuation (already heralded in Johann Abraham Peter Schulz's article "Symphony" in Sulzer's own *General Theory of the Fine Arts*)[12] an annoying paradox. The idea of "absolute music"—as we may henceforth call independent instrumental music, even though the term did not arise for another half-century—consists of the conviction that instrumental music purely and clearly expresses the true nature of music by its very lack of concept, object, and purpose. Not its existence, but what it stands for, is decisive. Instrumental music, as pure "structure," represents itself. Detached from the affections and feelings of the real world, it forms a "separate world for itself."[13] It is no coincidence that E. T. A. Hoffmann, who was the first to speak emphatically of music as "structure,"[14] proclaimed that instrumental music was the true music: that, in a sense, language in music therefore represented an addition "from without." "When speaking of music as an independent art, one should always mean instrumental music alone, which, disdaining any aid or admixture of another art, expresses the characteristic nature of art which is only recognizable within music itself."[15]

The idea that instrumental music devoid of function or program is the "true" music has since been eroded to a commonplace that determines the day-to-day use of music without our being aware of it, let alone doubting it. But when it was new it must have seemed a challenging paradox, for it bluntly contradicted an older idea of music established in a tradition that spanned millenia. What may seem obvious today, as though indicated in the nature of the thing—that music is a sounding phenomenon and nothing more, that a text is therefore considered an "extramusical" impetus—proves to be a historically molded theorem no more than two centuries old. Understanding the historical character of the idea serves two purposes: first, to prepare for the insight that what has come about historically can also be changed again; second, to understand more precisely the nature of today's predominant conception of music by becoming aware of its origins, i.e., the assumptions that underlie it, and of the background against which it sets itself off.

The older idea of music, against which the idea of absolute music had to prevail, was the concept, originating in antiquity and never doubted until the seventeenth century, that music, as Plato put it, consisted of *harmonia*, *rhythmos*, and *logos*. *Harmonia* meant regular, rationally systematized relationships among tones; *rhythmos*, the system of musical time, which in ancient times included dance and organized motion; and *logos*, language as the expression of human reason. Music without language was therefore reduced, its nature constricted: a deficient type or mere shadow of what music actually is. (Using a concept of music that includes language, one can justify not only vocal but even program music: it does not appear as a secondary application of literature to "absolute" music, nor is the program an addition "from without," but a reminder of the logos that music should always include in order to be its whole self.)

According to Arnold Schering (who still adhered even in the twentieth century to the older concept of music, which explains his tendency to discover "hidden programs" in Beethoven's symphonies), not until around 1800 "does the pernicious spectre of dualism between 'applied' (depen-

dent) and 'absolute' music enter European musical awareness, leading to serious conflicts. Thereafter there is no
longer a *single* concept of music, as previous generations
knew it, but *two*, about whose rank and historical priority
one soon begins to quarrel, just as one disputes the question
of the boundaries between them and their definition."[16]
One cannot speak of an unbroken dominance of the idea of
absolute music. Despite Haydn and Beethoven, mistrust of
absolute instrumental music independent of language had
not yet receded among nineteenth-century estheticians such
as Hegel and, later, Gervinus, Heinrich Bellerman, and
Eduard Grell. They suspected the "artificiality" of instrumental music of being a deviation from the "natural," or its
"conceptlessness" a renunciation of "reason." The traditional prejudice was deep-rooted: that music had to depend
on words to avoid either degeneration into pleasant noise
that neither touched the heart nor employed the mind, or
becoming an impenetrable spirit language. And insofar as
one did not reject "absolute music"—i.e., instrumental
music that both disdained tone painting and was not to
be perceived as the "language of the heart"—one sought
refuge in a hermeneutics that forced upon "pure, absolute
music" just what it sought to avoid: programs and char-
acterizations. If instrumental music had been a "pleasant
noise" *beneath* language to the common-sense estheticians
of the eighteenth century, then the romantic metaphysics of
art declared it a language *above* language. The urge to
include it in the central sphere of language could not be
suppressed.

And yet the idea of absolute music—gradually and
against resistance—became the esthetic paradigm of German musical culture in the nineteenth century. Whereas a
glance at repertoires and catalogues of works would deny
any superficial predominance of instrumental music in the
romantic and post-romantic periods, it is just as undeniable
that the concept of music in that era was ever more
decidedly molded by the esthetic of absolute music. (Except

for opera and some oratorios and songs, instrumental music predominates today, but this reflection of historical impact should not obscure the former prevalence of vocal music.) When even Hanslick's opponents called the text in vocal music an "extramusical" influence, the battle against "formalism" was lost even before it began, for Hanslick had already prevailed in the vocabulary with which they opposed him. (At first, the rise to predominance of "pure, absolute music" as a paradigm of musical thought was not at all correlated with the decay of literary culture the way it was in the twentieth century. In fact, as we shall demonstrate, the idea of absolute music in the first half of the nineteenth century was entwined with an esthetic driven by the concept of the "poetic"—the epitome not of the "literary," but of a substance common to the various arts. In the esthetics of Schopenhauer, Wagner, and Nietzsche, i.e., the reigning theory of art in the second half of the century, music was considered to be an expression of the "essence" of things, as opposed to the language of concepts that cleaved to mere "appearances." Although this was a triumph of the idea of absolute music within the doctrine of music drama, it by no means signified that poetry, as the mere vehicle of music, deserved neglect.)

The symphony was used as a prototype for the development of the theory of absolute music around 1800, viz. Wackenroder's "Psychology of Modern Instrumental Music,"[17] Tieck's essay "Symphonies,"[18] or E. T. A. Hoffmann's sketch of a romantic metaphysics of music that forms the introduction to a review of Beethoven's Fifth Symphony.[19] And when Daniel Schubart, as early as 1791, praised a piece of instrumental music with words that remind one of E. T. A. Hoffmann's dithyrambs for Beethoven, it was likewise a symphony that kindled his enthusiasm, albeit one by Christian Cannabich: "It is not the mere din of voices . . . it is a musical whole whose parts, like emanations of spirit, form a whole again."[20] The discussion of that time does not include chamber music. As Gottfried Wilhelm Fink wrote as late as 1838 in Gustav Schilling's *Encyclopedia of All Musical Sciences*, the "acknowledged apex of instrumental music" was the symphony.[21]

On the other hand, those writers' interpretations of the symphony as "language of a spirit world," "mysterious Sanskrit," or hieroglyphics were not the only attempt to understand the nature of absolute, object- and concept-free instrumental music. When Paul Bekker, writing during the German republican fervor of 1918, explained the symphony by the composer's intention "to speak, through instrumental music, to a multitude,"[22] he was, presumably without knowing it, reverting to an exegesis that stems from the classical period. Heinrich Christoph Koch's *Musical Lexicon* of 1802 (i.e., even before the *Eroica*) stated: "Because instrumental music is nothing but the imitation of song, the symphony especially represents the choir, and thus, like the choir, has the purpose of expressing the sentiment of a multitude."[23] Contrary to the romantics, who discovered the "true" music in instrumental music, Koch, a music theorist of the classical period, upheld the older interpretation that instrumental music was an "abstraction" of vocal music, and not the reverse, that vocal music was "applied" instrumental music. (The *Allgemeine Musikalische Zeitung* wrote in 1801 that Carl Philipp Emanuel Bach had demonstrated that "pure music was not merely a shell for applied music, nor an abstraction of it.")[24]

E. T. A. Hoffmann's famous remark that the symphony had become, "so to speak, the opera of the instruments" (which Fink still quoted in 1838) seems at first glance to express something similar to Koch's characterization.[25] However, one would misinterpret Hoffmann by maintaining that in 1809, a year before the review of Beethoven's Fifth Symphony, he was still convinced that vocal models were required for the esthetic comprehension of instrumental forms. Hoffmann is actually saying that the symphony's rank within instrumental music compares to that of the opera within vocal music; furthermore, he suggests that the symphony is like a "musical drama."[26] This concept of a drama of the instruments points to Wackenroder and Tieck,[27] whose *Fantasies on Art* Hoffmann seems to follow. It means nothing but the variety (or, as Tieck put it, the "beautiful confusion") of musical characters in a symphonic movement. However, the chaos of affections, which Christian Gottfried Körner opposed with a demand for unity of character,[28] is only a superficial phenomenon. Although a hasty glance creates the impression of an "utter lack of true unity and inner coherence, . . . a deeper vision is rewarded by the growth of a beautiful tree, buds and leaves, blossoms and fruit springing from its seed."[29] To Hoffmann, this is the common trait of the Beethovenian symphony and the Shakespearean drama, the latter being the romantic paradigm of the drama.[30] The remark about "drama of the instruments" is thus an esthetic analogy meant to indicate, by reference to Shakespeare, the "high thoughtfulness" behind the seeming disorder of the symphony.

Fink, in 1838, hesitantly accepted the description of the symphony as "opera of the instruments," but he transformed—or, as thought, distilled—it into a characterization: that "the grand symphony [was] comparable to a dramatized sentimental novella." "It is a dramatically expressed story, developed in a psychological context, told in tones, of some sentimental state of a community that, stimulated by a central impetus, expresses its essential feeling in every kind of popular representation individually through each instrument taken into the whole."[31] Fink's prototype for his description, eclectic in its mixture of lyric, epic, and dramatic elements, is obviously Beethoven's *Eroica*. The same work inspired Adolph Bernhard Marx in 1859 to his theory of "ideal music." (One could assert, with a certain amount of exaggeration, that the romantic-"poetic" exegesis referred to the Fifth Symphony, the

Young Hegelian "characterizing" exegesis to the Third, and the New German School's "programmatic" exegesis to the Ninth.) According to Marx, the *Eroica* is "that piece in which musical art first steps independently—without connection to the poet's word or the dramatist's action—out of the play of form and uncertain impulses and feelings and into the sphere of brighter, more certain consciousness, in which it comes of age and takes its place as a peer in the circle of its sisters."[32] (Music's "equality of rank" with poetry and painting was also a central theme in Liszt's apologia for program music.) This construction, a matter of esthetics and philosophy of history, that supports Marx's interpretation of Beethoven, is based on the threefold scheme of faculty psychology, a division of mental powers into senses, feelings, and mind. Thus Marx sees the mere "play of tones" as a first, primitive stage of development, and the "uncertain impulses and feelings" as a second and higher one that nevertheless must be surpassed. Only by transition from the "sphere of feelings" to that of the "idea" does music reach its predestined goal. "This was Beethoven's accomplishment."[33] Music history is consummated in the *Eroica*. However, an "idea"—of which a symphony must be the "material manifestation" in order to elevate itself to art in the emphatic sense—is none other than a "portrait progressing in psychological, inexorable development."[34] Marx, in the spirit of Young Hegelianism, brings romantic metaphysics down to earth.

"Portrait"[35]—a term recurring in Friedrich Theodor Vischer's *Esthetics* as a characteristic of the symphony—appears as the key word in a theory of the symphony that represents a counterproject to the "poetics" of absolute music. First, Marx trivialized the concept of "absolute" music "dissolved" from functions, texts, and finally even affections—a concept that both the Young Hegelians and the New German School found useless for Beethoven interpretation—into the idea of a "merely formal" music reduced to its sensual force, in which—by a strange projection of faculty psychology onto history—he claimed to perceive a first stage in the development of music. Second, the musically spiritual, which romantic metaphysics found expressed in the "pure, absolute musical art" (as an "intimation of the infinite," the absolute), was claimed by Marx for "characteristic" music, and by Brendel even for "program" music, in which one perceived "progress" from the expression of "indefinite" feelings to the representation of "definite" ideas. (Marx's esthetics undeniably attached itself to an authentic tradition: the tendency toward "characterization" in Körner's sense, which belonged to the principal features of the classical symphony, Beethoven's as well as Haydn's.) Rather than in the ethereal "poetic," Marx sought the nature of the symphony in the firmly outlined "characteristic" mode, Brendel even in the detailed "programmatic" one. (The metaphysics of instrumental music, which seemed dead and buried in 1850, soon celebrated its resurrection in the Schopenhauer renaissance brought about by Wagner and later by Nietzsche.)

That the symphony and not the string quartet (as the epitome of chamber music) represented the intuitive model for the development of the idea of absolute music stems less from the nature of the music than from the nature of the esthetic writings in question. As publicity, they were oriented to the symphony as a form of public concert; the string quartet, which belonged to a private musical culture, was overshadowed. Beethoven, albeit hesitantly, had already sought the transition to a public style of quartet at the beginning of the century: in Op. 59 the change in social character is part of the composition, as it were; on the other hand, the *Quartetto Serioso*, Op. 95 was originally intended to remain withheld from the public. Even so, Robert Schumann, in his "Second Matinée of Quartets" (1838), could still call a piece by Karl Gottlieb Reissiger "a quartet to be heard by bright candlelight, among beautiful women,"—i.e., a salon piece—"whereas real Beethovenians lock the door, imbibing and reveling in every single measure."[36] In the 1830s, "Beethovenians" were not simply adherents of Beethoven, but those who also, and above all, venerated the late works. However, abstruseness characterized the string quartet just when it completely expressed the nature of "pure, absolute musical art" instead of tending toward salon music, as Reissiger's piece did. Thus public awareness was inhibited in connecting the idea of absolute music, which was more current among literati than among musicians, to a genre that, by internal criteria, must have seemed predestined for such a connection. Carl Maria von Weber's comment on quartets by Friedrich Ernst Fesca is also typical: just by choosing the genre, the composer demonstrated that one could "count him among the few who, in these times that often tend toward shallowness in art, is still serious about studying the innermost essence of art."[37] On the other hand, he describes the "quartet style" as "belonging more to the social, domestically serious sphere."[38] In other words: the "innermost essence of art" reveals itself where one secludes oneself from the world, from the public.

Ferdinand Hand's *Esthetics of Art* is historically significant insofar as, lacking the prejudice of philosophical demands or unusual musical judgments, it represents the "normal awareness," so to speak, of educated people around 1840. Although he still saw the "culmination" of instrumental music in the symphony,[39] he praised the string quartet as "the flower of the new music: for it erects the purest result of harmony . . . Whoever has penetrated the nature and effect of harmony will on the one hand consider Weber's calling it the cerebral element of music completely justified, and on the other hand recognize the totality of mental activity with which such a work is both created by the artist and received by the listener."[40] ("Harmony" is to be understood as a synonym for "strict composition," the artificial part of music.) For a time, the symphony, the "drama of the instruments," still appears as the highest genre of instrumental music (analogous to the drama in the poetics of the nineteenth century). But if the string quartet represents the "cerebral in music," then it must gradually become the epitome of absolute music, growing in proportion to the decline of metaphysical import (the intimation of the absolute) in favor of the specifically esthetic component of the idea (the thought that form in music is spirit and spirit in music is form).

According to Karl Köstlin, who wrote the specifically music-theoretical sections of Friedrich Theodor Vischer's *Esthetics*, the string quartet is "a thought-music of pure art:" "both sides, the formal and the material"—i.e., the artificial, artistic one and the "shadowy" one of sound— "are finally united in one and the same result, namely in that this music"—the string quartet—"is the most intellectual kind; it leads us out of the din of life and into the still, shadowy realm of the ideal,"—the accepted metaphysics of the beginning of the century has paled to a comforting fiction —"into the non-material world of the mind that has withdrawn into itself, into its most secret affective life, and that internally confronts that affective life. It realizes just this ideal side of instrumental music; it is a thought-music of pure art, from which, to be sure, we soon desire to return to the full reality of forms more naturalistically rich in sound."[41] In the term "pure art," as Köstlin uses it, an older meaning—"art" as the epitome of the technical, artificial, and learned, of strict composition—flows into a new one: "art" as artistic character in the sense of the esthetic nature of music. The history of the word reflects an intellectual and social change: in the 1850s—Hanslick published his treatise *The Beautiful in Music* in 1854—"pure art" in the formal sense, which had always been conceded to the string quartet, was accepted also as "pure art" in the esthetic sense, as a pure realization of the "material appearance of the idea" (Hegel).

Although Hanslick's muting of the romantic metaphysics

of instrumental music to an esthetics of the "specifically musical," combined with the axiom that form in music was spirit, gave the "purely formal" string quartet the chance to appear as the paradigm of "pure, absolute music," this does not mean that the metaphysical side of the idea of absolute music had been extinguished: it reappeared in the Schopenhauerian renaissance, brought about by Wagner, starting in the 1860s. Moreover, in Beethoven's late quartets, which—not least due to the efforts of the Müller brothers—were entering the public's musical consciousness around that time, the artificial, esoteric motive is inseparable from the motive of metaphysical intimation. To Nietzsche, they therefore represent the purest expression of absolute music: "The highest revelations of music make us perceive, even involuntarily, the crudity of all imagery, and of every affect chosen for analogy; e.g., as the last Beethoven quartets put every perception, and for that matter, the entire realm of empirical reality, to shame. In the presence of the highest god, truly revealing himself," — i.e., Dionysus—"the symbol has no meaning anymore: truly, it now seems to be an offensive triviality."[42] Around 1870, Beethoven's quartets became the paradigm of the idea of absolute music that had been created around 1800 as a theory of the symphony: the idea that music is a revelation of the absolute, specifically because it "dissolves" itself from the sensual, and finally even from the affective sphere.

2

The History of the Term
and Its Vicissitudes

The history of the term is itself quite strange. The expression was coined, not by Eduard Hanslick, as is always claimed, but by Richard Wagner; and the tortuous dialectic obscured by a façade of apologetic and polemical formulas in Wagner's esthetics determined the development of the concept of absolute music into the twentieth century.

In the "program" to Beethoven's Ninth Symphony that Wagner pieced together in 1846 from *Faust* quotations and esthetic commentaries, we read of the instrumental recitative of the fourth movement: "Already almost breaking the bounds of absolute music, it stems the tumult of the other instruments with its virile eloquence, pressing toward decision, and passes at last into a song-like theme."[1] The "decision" Wagner means is the transition from "imprecise," objectless instrumental music to objectively "precise" vocal music. Wagner ascribes "endless and imprecise expressiveness" to pure instrumental music; in a footnote he quotes Ludwig Tieck, who perceived in symphonies "insatiate desire forever hieing forth and turning back into itself."[2] The theory of instrumental music to which Wagner subscribed when speaking of absolute music was romantic metaphysics. But "endless and imprecise expressiveness," instead of functioning as the language of a spirit world, was to be transformed into a finite and precise one, to be brought down to earth, as it were. "The first thing, the beginning and basis of all that is extant or conceivable, is true physical being."[3]

However, Wagner's esthetic is riddled with discontinuities. His language betrays contradiction: his reference to "limitations" to absolute music, while he also says that it expresses the "infinite," is the sign of a divided judgment. In the introduction to the "program," Wagner emphasizes that the *Faust* quotations do not define the "meaning" of the Ninth Symphony, but merely evoke an analogous "spiritual ambience"; because a hermeneutics that is aware of its limitations must concede that "the essence of higher instrumental music consists in its uttering in tones a thing unspeakable in words."[4] This argument is not openly contradictory: one may perceive programs as insufficient, as not approaching the "nature of higher instrumental music," and still praise the transition from instrumental to vocal music as the "redemption" of "tone" by the "word." On the other hand, if the indefinite nature of instrumental music is first elevated to the expression of what is verbally "inexpressible"—which, in the tradition of the topos of unspeakability, means the "higher" values—only to be characterized as "imprecise" and driving toward "precision," the change in valuation is unmistakable. "Bold, wordless music," as Wackenroder calls it, is once again, as in the earlier part of the eighteeenth century, demoted below vocal music.

Some years later, in *Art of the Future* (1849) and *Opera and Drama* (1851), the term "absolute music," which had been inconspicuous and isolated in the "program"—or the class of terms that includes the expressions "absolute music," "absolute instrumental music," "absolute musical language," "absolute melody," and "absolute harmony"—becomes the central word in a historical-philosophical or historical-mythological construction that leads to the music drama. With polemical accent, Wagner calls "absolute" all "partial arts" torn away from the "total work of art." (Wagner calls pantomime, wordless and

19

emancipated from the drama, the "mute, absolute play.")[5] The coloration of the word "absolute" has been changed, clearly under the influence of the philosophy of Ludwig Feuerbach, as Klaus Kropfinger recognized.[6] "Absolute music," according to Wagner, is "detached" music, severed from its roots in speech and dance, and thus simply abstract. Hoping that the music drama would provide a rebirth of Greek tragedy, he reverted to the music-esthetic paradigm of ancient origin from which romantic metaphysics had distanced itself polemically in the late eighteenth century. In order to truly be music in the unrestricted sense of the word, *harmonia* (the coherence of tones) must remain combined with *rhythmos* and *logos*, i.e., with ordered movement and language. To Wagner this means: in the music drama, music cooperates with scenic action— i.e., bodily movement—and with the poetic text, and only thus attains the perfection denied absolute music. The "total work of art" is pointedly the "true music"; in contrast, absolute music, detached from its establishment and justification through speech and action, is a deficient type.

The urge to restore the "ancient truth" (from which came revolutionary consequences, as with Monteverdi and Gluck) in no way represents a denial of the immediate tradition. Wagner, in the "program" of 1846, on the one hand sought support in the romantic metaphysics of the symphony so that, on the other hand, he might go beyond it (based on the choral finale). Likewise, the idea shared by Wackenroder, Tieck, and E. T. A. Hoffmann is not extinguished, but rather sublimated in Wagner's reform writings of ca. 1850; they contributed the term "absolute music" to the idea, albeit with polemical intent.

Art of the Future is dedicated to Ludwig Feuerbach, the title of whose book *Foundations of the Philosophy of the Future* (1843) Wagner was alluding to or parodying.[7] Furthermore, Wagner's discussion of Beethoven's "absolute music" is strikingly analogous to Feuerbach's discussion of "absolute philosophy."[8] "Absolute philosophy" is Hegel's speculative thought, polemically distorted by Feuerbach's perspective as an anthropologically oriented philosopher who sought to return philosophy from high-flown metaphysics to the empirics of human physical existence. "Absolute philosophy" is a philosophy of the "absolute," interpreted or denounced as severed from its roots in earthly and human matters, and thus "absolute" in a different sense. Metaphysical pretension is to be exposed as a fiction; and the double meaning of the word "absolute" becomes the linguistic vehicle of the polemics against Hegelian speculation. But Feuerbach does not simply deny the religious-metaphysical content that Hegel had formulated, or declare it vacuous; instead he returns it, in a sense, to the physical human as an "inheritance" that had been "alienated" from him by theological and philosophical dogmas. The immediate tradition, that of metaphysics, is thus sublimated, as in Wagner's theory of instrumental music: retained, but transformed, and in just that way actually returned to itself.

Wagner characterized Rossini's operatic style as "absolute melody," music with its roots in the air. Whereas Heine had perceived the music of Rossini as expression of the spirit (or lack of spirit) of the Restoration period, Wagner drew a sneering parallel between the "absolute monarchy" of Metternich's state and "absolute melody."[9] In deriding the opera aria, "detached from all linguistic or poetic basis," he did not shrink even from such epithets as "lifeless, spiritless trifles of fashion," "repulsive," and "indescribably hideous."[10]

Aside from instrumental music, the concept of absolute music therefore includes vocal music that hovers over its words, "detached from all linguistic or poetic basis." On the other hand, instrumental music is not strictly absolute as long as it retains some influence of the dance. (Wagner's terminology is not completely consistent, however, and could hardly have been so, for the expression "absolute music" is a negative, collective term determined by its antithesis to "music drama": instrumental music is "absolute" insofar as it is "dissolved" from the dance, but also in that the dance, whose form it preserves, is "torn from" the "music drama.")

"Absolute instrumental music" as Wagner understood it is, strictly speaking, music "no longer" determined by the dance and "not yet" determined by speech and scenic action. The "infinite longing" that E. T. A. Hoffmann felt Beethoven's symphonies expressed appears to Wagner as awareness or feeling of an unfortunate intermediate state, in which the origin of instrumental music is lost, and the future goal not yet attained. Thus Wagner in no way denied the romantic metaphysics of the symphony, but reinterpreted it: rather than a goal of music history, it was a mere antithesis, an intermediate step in a dialectic process. As such it is as unavoidable as it is preliminary. "After Haydn and Mozart, there could and had to be a Beethoven; the genius of music necessarily demanded him, and he appeared without delay; who will now be to Beethoven what he was to Haydn and Mozart in the area of absolute music? The greatest genius would no longer be able to accomplish anything here, simply because the genius of absolute music no longer requires him."[11]

To be sure, Wagner felt that Beethoven had gone beyond the "absolute-musical" in the "second half" of his oeuvre (i.e., after the *Eroica*),[12] insofar as he had striven to transform the "endless and imprecise expressiveness" that limits pure instrumental music into a precise, finite one.[13] In so doing, Wagner entangled himself in the following philosophical difficulty: in searching for a false, unreachable goal, that of extracting an individuated, objectively determined expressiveness from instrumental music, Beethoven discovered musical means that later made it possible to attain the true goal of the history of music—a vocal music that not only accompanied and illustrated speech, but also "realized it for the senses."

If one takes Wagner's historical constructs at face value, then the force of absolute instrumental music that expresses "infinite longing" seems to approach the vanishing point. Earlier symphonic writing (still including Beethoven's Seventh Symphony as "apotheosis of the dance") is not completely "dissolved" from instrumental music's roots in the dance; on the other hand, the *Eroica* and Fifth Symphonies, in groping for (but not attaining) individualized, objectively determined expression, already go beyond the "absolute-musical"; and the choral finale of the Ninth Symphony consummately represents the "redemption" of "tone" by the "word." Absolute instrumental music is thus less a firmly outlined genre than a dialectical force in the music-historical development that drives toward the music drama, toward the rebirth of tragedy.

In Wagner's view of historical reality, absolute instrumental music seen as expression of the "infinite" hardly ever appeared in unadulterated form. This did not stop him from appropriating E. T. A. Hoffmann's idea that the symphony captures the spirit of the modern Christian era in tones, albeit with a historical-philosophical twist foreign to Hoffmann: paganism, with which Wagner, as a follower of Feuerbach, identified, allowed him to speak of Christian music as a sublimated force in the dialectic of music history.

In *Art of the Future* we read: "We must not yet abandon our image of the sea for the nature of musical art. If rhythm and melody"—music dependent on dance and words, respectively—"are the shores on which music touches and fertilizes the two continents of the arts that share its origin"—the concept of dance includes dramatic action and gesticulation—"then sound is its liquid, innate element; but the immeasurable extent of this liquid is the sea of harmony. The eye recognizes only the surface of this sea: only the depths of the heart understand its depths."[14] Wagner praises "absolute harmony"[15] in language indistinguishable from the metaphysical excesses of Tieck, Wack-

enroder, and E. T. A. Hoffmann, excesses that clash with
the tone of Feuerbachian anthropology. "Man dives into
this sea in order to return to daylight refreshed and
beautiful; his heart feels wonderfully expanded when he
looks down into this depth, capable of all the most
inconceivable possibilities, whose bottom his eye shall never
fathom, whose unfathomableness thereby fills him with
wonder and intimations of the infinite."[16] However, the
metaphysics of "absolute harmony" is not the last word
about the "nature of music"; instead, it is drawn into a
historical dialectic that aims toward music drama, the
"redemption" of "tone" by the "word." Wagner develops
his metaphor further: "When the Hellene sailed his sea, he
never lost sight of the coastland: it was to him the safe
current that bore him from shore to shore, on which he
rode between the familiar beaches to the melodic rhythm of
the oars—turning here his eye to the dance of the wood
nymphs, there his ear to the hymn of the gods, whose
meaningfully melodic tune of words carried to him the
atmosphere of the temple from the mountain heights."[17] In
the ancient world, *harmonia*, instead of being "absolute,"
was bound to *rhythmos* ("the dance of the wood nymphs")
and to *logos* ("the hymn of the gods"). In contrast, the
music of the Christian era is, conceptually, "absolute
harmony"; within that concept, to Wagner as to E. T. A.
Hoffmann, Palestrina's vocal polyphony and modern instrumental music overlap strangely in a historical-philosophical sense, however awkwardly they might relate to one
another in musical reality. "The Christian parted from the
shores of life . . . Farther and more unbounded he sought
out the seas in order finally to be completely alone in the
ocean, between the sea and the heavens."[18] But Christian
harmony, however sublime it may be, is to be replaced by
the melody of neo-heathen drama: a melody for which
Beethoven developed the musical means without recognizing their true purpose. (What was attained in the sym-

phony, in which Christian harmony perfected itself, is sublimated in the drama of the future, to which the symphony unconsciously aspired.) "But in Nature, everything measureless struggles for measure; all that is unbounded draws boundaries for itself . . . just as Columbus taught us to sail the ocean and thus connect all the continents, so were new, undreamt-of shores attained by the hero who plied the wide, shoreless sea of absolute music to its boundaries . . . and this hero is none other than Beethoven."[19] (Wagner wielded the Columbus metaphor in various ways. In *Art of the Future* he means nothing other than that Columbus discovered America—that Beethoven groped forward to the "redemption" of "tone" by the "word" in the choral finale of the Ninth Symphony. But in *Opera and Drama*[20] he brings out the fact that Columbus lived his life under the misconception that America was India—that Beethoven's attempt to develop the musical means he had discovered, which belong in fact to the drama's language of word and tone, was driven entirely by his erroneous notion that these were the means of an individuating and objectively defined form of expression within a purely tonal language.)

However vigorously he may have accentuated it, the historical dialectic that moves toward the music drama in no way represents Wagner's whole esthetic. What the "image of the sea" expresses, i.e., "absolute harmony," is, as Wagner says, the "essence of musical art." Moreover, the dichotomy between a philosophy of history that sees absolute music as antithesis and intermediate stage in a dialectic process, and an ontology in which, as "intimation of the infinite," absolute music touches the essence of things, remains unmitigated. The archaizing esthetic that tends to demote absolute music to a deficent type, and the romantic metaphysics that presents absolute music as the true music; the apologetic construct by which Wagner sought to elevate his own work to the goal of music history, and the romantic inheritance that secretly nourished his concept of music—the contradictions seem like a gaping abyss.

The contradiction returns in a different form in the open letter "On Franz Liszt's Symphonic Poems," in which Wagner used the term "absolute music" for the last time. "Hear ye my creed: never, nor in any combination into which it enters, can music cease to be the highest, most redeeming art." (Meanwhile, in 1854, Wagner had adopted Schopenhauer's metaphysics of music.) "But, obvious as this is, it is equally certain that music can only be understood in forms drawn from a relationship to life, or an expression of life, forms that, originally foreign to music, only receive their deepest meaning through music, as if through the revelation of the music latent in them." (Even after his conversion to Schopenhauer, Wagner did not want to surrender the thesis, from "Opera and Drama," that music was dependent on language and the dance for "form motives.") "There is nothing (N. B.: regarding its appearance in life) less absolute than music, and the defenders of an absolute music evidently do not know what they mean; to confound them one need only ask them to show us a music separate from the form that it took from movement or the meters of language (in a causal relationship)." (If one considers the difference between the genesis of a thing and its value, the remarks in parentheses are almost a contradiction of the rest: although music requires an external form motive for its existence, it is, in essence, absolute.) "Thus we agree on this point, and grant that, in this human world, the music of the gods required a binding or, as we have seen, a determining force in order to make its appearance possible."[21] The polemic against the term "absolute music," the term that Hanslick had meanwhile taken up (1854), must not obscure Wagner's latent affinity for the idea of absolute music. Music, in an empirical sense, "in this human world," may require a basic formal motive in order to take shape, but this does not exclude the possibility that in a metaphysical sense, as "divine music," it expresses the "innermost nature of the world," to paraphrase Schopenhauer. Empirically "qualified," music "qualifies" in the metaphysical world. Wagner, it seems, was hindered from taking the step of designating the symphonic "orchestral melody," which constitutes the nature and substance of the music drama, as "absolute music" only because he was committed to a polemical use of the word, aimed at Rossini and Meyerbeer, or to a critical-dialetic one that related the Beethovenian symphony to his philosophy of history. In addition, Hanslick had incorporated the term into the context of a theory of the "specifically musical" that Wagner necessarily saw as being opposed to both his Feuerbach-inspired and his Schopenhauer-inspired esthetics.

Thus Wagner spoke of Beethoven's absolute instrumental music in the dithyrambic tones of romanticism, in order to declare it a mere intermediate step that the musical spirit of the age must surpass on the way to music drama; Hanslick, in appropriating Wagner's term "absolute musical art," did just the opposite, reverting to E. T. A. Hoffmann's thesis that pure instrumental music was the "true" music and represented the goal of the history of music, even as he toned the romantic metaphysics of the symphony down to an esthetic of the "specifically musical"—an esthetic presented in an attitude of dry empiricism in the spirit of disenchantment after the collapse of Hegelianism around 1850. "Of that which instrumental music cannot do, let it never be said that music can achieve it; for instrumental music alone is pure, absolute music."[22]

Though it may seem that for Hanslick the term "absolute music" had completely sacrificed its metaphysical aura and expressed nothing but the claim of textless, functionless, and programless music to being "true music," this is at least partially deceptive. The first edition of the treatise *The Beautiful in Music* (1854) closes with a dithyramb that betrays the "formalist" Hanslick's piety toward the romantic metaphysics of instrumental music. (One may sense, but not prove, that "believed" metaphysics has been muted to an "edifying" symbolism here.) "This spiritual content thus combines, in the soul of the listener, the beautiful in music with all other great and beautiful ideas. He does not experience music merely as bare and absolute through its own beauty, but simultaneously as a sounding image of the great movements in the universe. Through deep and secret relationships to nature the meaning of tones is heightened far beyond the tones themselves, and allows us always to feel the infinite even as we listen to the work of human talent. Just as the elements of music-sound, tone, rhythm, strength, weakness—are found in the entire universe, so man rediscovers in music the entire universe."[23] After a review by Robert Zimmermann ("It seems to us superfluous that, as Hanslick proceeds, these pure tone relationships reveal something besides themselves, e.g. rise to an intimation of the absolute. The absolute is not a tone relationship and thus, we think, not musical"),[24] Hanslick decided to omit the final paragraph, as well as an analogous passage in the third chapter to which Zimmermann alludes in the passage quoted.[25] But it would be erroneous to view this renunciation as an admission that a mere philosophical ornament was at stake, whose deletion did not influence the structure of the argument; for even a quick examination of the prehistory of music-esthetic "formalism" shows that especially Hanslick's central category, the concept of form perfected in itself, was closely related to the interpretation of music as metaphor for the universe in the development of that esthetic. The unspoken argument that operated in the background of Hanslick's work, combining the concept of musical form with music's metaphysical claim, was developed in Karl Philipp Moritz's treatise "On the Visual Imitation of the Beautiful" of 1788 and August Wilhelm Schlegel's 1801 Berlin *Lectures on Fine Arts and Literature*. According to Moritz, a work of art, insofar as it fulfills no external purpose (i.e., a practical, moral, or sentimental one) and exists instead for its own sake, is a "whole perfected in itself" that, as Schelling put it, lingers in the "sublime indifference of the beautiful." Actually, the only whole that is perfected in itself is all of nature—the universe. And art, to attain closure, must appear as image and analogy of all of nature. "For this great coherence of nature is, after all, the only true whole; because of the indissoluble concatenation of things, any isolated whole within it is merely *eingebildet*—*eingebildet* here means both "fictive" and "infused (Latin: *informatus*) with this quality through the genius"—but even that which is *eingebildet* must, when viewed as a whole, resemble that great whole as we conceive of it, and be formed by the eternal, firm rules according to which it (the particular, *eingebildet* object) supports itself from all sides at its center and rests on its own Being."[26] By way of the idea of the object complete within itself, Moritz thus combined the idea of the autonomy of art, of its independence from function, with the interpretation of the work of art as a metaphor for the universe.

This does not mean, however, that in order to understand Hanslick's music-esthetic concept of form one must revert to the metaphysics of art of Goethe's time. But this backward glance at Moritz's category of the object complete within itself should suffice to make plausible the notion that Hanslick's metaphysical digression (suppressed from the second edition onward) *can* be tied to the central thesis that musical form is "thought forming itself from the inside out,"[27] even though the connection is suggested more by the adjacency of the tradition than by compelling logic. Hanslick's concept of "absolute musical art" also hides a metaphysical implication that was later made explicit: that music, specifically by "dissolving" itself from functions, texts, and programs as pure instrumental music, can appear as an image of the "absolute." Half a century later, August Halm took up and further defined the emphatic concept of form that represented Hanslick's decisive step beyond the romantic metaphysics of instrumental music; following Halm, Ernst Kurth combined the idea with a concept of "absolute music" that was exalted into the realm of the immeasurable, a concept that owed its pathos partly to the memory of the romantic era and partly to the esthetic of Schopenhauer and Nietzsche that dominated around 1900 (Kurth was born in 1886).

As we have mentioned, Wagner's open letter "On Franz Liszt's Symphonic Poems" is disjointed in that the obvious polemic against the term "absolute music" creates a rhetorical façade behind which hides a latent affinity to the idea of absolute music, an idea that had been transmitted to Wagner first through Tieck and then through Schopenhauer—who had himself received the romantic esthetic. The same disjunction can be seen in a different form in Friedrich Nietzsche at the beginning of the 1870s, at a time when his friendship with Wagner was still unclouded. The treatises that Nietzsche published to Wagner's greater glory, *The Birth of Tragedy out of the Spirit of Music* (1871), and *Richard Wagner in Bayreuth* (1876), do not speak of "absolute music." However, an unpublished fragment called "On Music and Word," which apparently dates from 1871, says: "What are we to make of that enormous esthetic superstition: that Beethoven himself, with that fourth movement of the Ninth, made a solemn statement about the limits of absolute music, yea, unlocked the portals of a new art in which music could even represent images and concepts, and thus became accessible to the 'conscious spirit'?"[28] The polemic is obviously directed against Wagner's interpretation of Beethoven in *Opera and Drama* and *Art of the Future*, even though the immediate object of the attack is Franz Brendel's apologia for Liszt.

The fundamental esthetic theorem from which Wagner proceeded in *Opera and Drama*—pointed polemically against the operatic tradition—declared music to be a function of the drama. "The error in the artistic genre of opera lay in the fact that a means of expression (music) became the purpose, and the purpose of the expression (the drama) was made into a means."[29] Therefore, Nietzsche is consciously contradicting and challenging Wagner when he writes in the fragment "On Music and Word" that it is "a curious arrogance" that places music "in the service of a series of images and concepts, to use it as a means to an end, to amplify and clarify them."[30] (Here, as above, Brendel's theory of program music is the intended target; this hardly changes the fact that Wagner's esthetic of music drama is likewise affected by the critique, which Nietzsche must have known.) Nietzsche's objection means nothing less than that music is not the medium of the drama, but that, inversely, the drama is expression and analogy of the music. Schopenhauer was "quite right to characterize drama in relation to music as a schema, as an example of a general concept."[31] The nature of things, says Nietzsche, resounds from music; drama merely reproduces their appearance. Whereas Wagner understood "drama" to be primarily scenic action—"not the dramatic poem, but the drama that actually moves before our eyes"[32] —Nietzsche denigrates the theatre: "In this sense, opera is naturally, at best, good music and only music: whereas the stunts performed at the same time are merely a fantastic disguise for the orchestra, above all for its most important instruments, the singers; a disguise from which those with insight turn away laughing."[33]

The situation in intellectual history documented in Nietzsche's fragment "On Music and Words" is confusingly paradoxical. The disdainful gesture with which the theatre is dismissed anticipates a central motive of later Wagner criticism, namely the accusation of being "like an actor" and "false." In "Nietzsche contra Wagner," the apostate's lampooning, he writes: "One sees that I am anti-theatrically minded; in the depths of my soul, I have the deepest scorn for the theatre, the mass art par excellence, that every true artist of today has."[34] "We know the masses; we know the theatre."[35] On the other hand, the deprecation of scenic—and verbal—elements of the opera derive from Schopenhauer's esthetic, which Nietzsche, backed by Wagner's enthusiasm for Schopenhauer, took up and expressed pointedly, and applied to *Tristan*, although Schopenhauer had expounded it in praise of Rossini—in praise of "absolute melody," to use Wagner's phrase. In *The World as Will and Representation* he writes that music "never expresses appearance, but only the inner nature, the of-itself of all appearance, the will itself . . . this is why our fantasy is so easily stimulated by it and thus attempts to form that spirit world that speaks to us so immediately, invisible and yet so vivid, and then tries to cloak it in flesh and bone, that is, to embody it in an analogous example. This is the origin of texted song and, ultimately, of opera—whose text, just for this reason, should never depart from this subordinate role and elevate itself to the forefront, making the music a mere means of expression; this is a great blunder and a dire perversion."[36] The "spirit world" to which Schopenhauer feels himself transported by music reminds one of E. T. A. Hoffmann's "Dschinnistan" and "Atlantis," and the outlines of Schopenhauer's esthetic are nothing other than the romantic metaphysics of absolute music philosophically interpreted in the context of a metaphysics of the "will."

Music, says Schopenhauer, provides the *universalia ante rem*,[37] using scholastic terminology (and Nietzsche appropriates the term).[38] Nietzsche also unmistakably drew the consequence that the substance of music drama is the "orchestral melody," the symphony—i.e., "absolute music" as expression of the "absolute," of the "will." *Tristan und Isolde*, the opus metaphysicum, might require action and a poetic text, but only because no listener could spiritually survive the work if it were presented as the symphony it actually is. "To these true musicians I direct the question: can they imagine a person capable of perceiving the third act of *Tristan und Isolde* purely as an immense symphonic movement, lacking any aid of words or scenery, without expiring from a paroxysmic undoing of all the wings of his soul?"[39] Nietzsche heard the music drama as a symphony; the rest is "stunts" or defenses. Thus he sustained the thesis that instrumental music was the "true" music — that of Wackenroder, Tieck, and E. T. A. Hoffmann, as translated via Schopenhauer — and applied it to Wagner's music drama (as Schopenhauer had applied it to Rossini's operas). The fact that music drama was originally based on the opposite paradigm, the conviction that music consisted of *harmonia*, *rhythmos*, and *logos*, sank into oblivion. On the other hand, Nietzsche had *Tristan* to thank for a musical experience that made palpable sense to him of what had been abstract speculation before: Schopenhauer's doctrine that music expresses "the innermost nature of the world." The idea of absolute music that E. T. A. Hoffmann had experienced in Beethoven's Fifth Symphony — related to Wackenroder and Tieck's metaphysics of instrumental music — was revealed to Nietzsche in Wagner's *Tristan*: the idea that music attains its metaphysical destiny in the very process of distancing itself ever further from empirical circumstances — from functions, words, plots, and finally even from humanly palpable feelings and affections.

At first Nietzsche used the term "absolute music" literally, applying it to the emancipation, the dissolution of music from language. "The music of every people certainly originates in conjunction with the lyric; and long before an absolute music can be conceived of, it passes, thus united, through the most important stages of development."[40] Absolute music, historically the later form, is metaphysically the original one. And, when stated affirmatively, the polemical statement that it is an "esthetic superstition" that the "boundaries of absolute music" were shown in the

Ninth Symphony means that there are no boundaries to absolute music. In Nietzsche's esthetic, Wagner's *Tristan* is absolute music.

Although Nietzsche, as the exegete of Wagner the composer, seems to be subjecting Wagner the theoretician to a rigorous critique, there was agreement around 1871 on esthetic principles that did not become altogether public only because Wagner shrank from unmistakably recanting the central theses of *Opera and Drama*. Two decades after *Opera and Drama*, he had long since stopped believing that music was, or needed to be, a function of the drama. In the 1870 essay on Beethoven, the central document of his reception of Schopenhauer, we read: "Music expresses the innermost nature of the gesture" — "gesture" being an abbreviation for scenic and mimetic action in general — "in a way so immediately comprehensible that, as soon as we are wholly fulfilled by music, even our face testifies to our intensive perception of the gesture, so that we finally understand it without seeing it ourselves."[41] The Feuerbach enthusiast, who accentuated the physical existence of the human being (e.g., the visible action within the drama), had become an adept of Schopenhauer, hearing the "innermost nature" of the music drama's action in the "orchestral melody." And the esthetic-dramaturgical agenda that Wagner had outlined before the composition of the *Ring* had been partially frustrated by the experience of composing *Tristan*. In the 1872 essay "On the Term 'Music Drama,' " Wagner calls his dramas "musical deeds become visible."[42] Music is the "nature" of which drama appears as the "physical manifestation," as Hegel would say. And in 1878, in an outburst of disgust at "the world of costume and makeup", he even speaks of the "invisible theatre" — analogous to the "invisible orchestra" — that one would need to invent.[43] The theatre enthusiast, disappointed by the realities of the theatre, withdrew into a fantasy, as Nietzsche had sketched in *The Birth of Tragedy*. But the "innermost nature" of that imagined theatre was the symphony; and the road Wagner took to the metaphysics of music was that much closer for being a return road, for, even in the reform writings of 1850, Wagner had preserved some affinity for the romantic metaphysics of instrumental music, even at the price of a disjuncture in his esthetic system. When calling music the substance on which drama feeds, he did not speak of "absolute music"; the memory of his polemical use of the term was not to be extinguished. But the idea for which he had found the term was, secretly, his idea too.

In colloquial music esthetics of the latter nineteenth century—which, like any other common parlance, made terms into slogans while neglecting the problems that constitute the life of those terms—the term "absolute music" appears as a vacuous label of "purely formal" instrumental music in contrast to both program music on the one hand, and vocal music. A characteristic use of the word is found in Ottokar Hostinsky's book *The Beautiful in Music and the Complete Art Work from the Viewpoint of Formal Esthetics*,[44] a book that attempted to mediate between Wagner and Hanslick. But Hostinsky did not seize the opportunity, latent in his argument, to develop a differentiated concept of absolute music.

Hostinsky sees Hanslick's esthetic of "pure, absolute musical art," the esthetics of the "specifically musical," as part of a more comprehensive system in which "absolute" instrumental music and vocal music with poetic-dramatic motivation receive equal rights as paradigms of music. Neither is absolute music the "true" music, as Hanslick had proclaimed, nor does it represent an earlier, lower stage of development. Hostinsky compares "absolute, purely formal, objectless"[45] music with architecture and ornamentation, and "representative, content-laden, objective" music with sculpture and painting, in order to demonstrate that there exist not one "pure musical art" but rather two possibilities of a "pure style" in music.[46] On the other hand, Hostinsky recognizes the distortion in the accusation that Wagner had "shattered" the musical forms; this recognition disturbs the simplicity of his esthetic system. He distinguishes three developmental stages or types: the "architectonic" form of "absolute" instrumental music; the decadent form of traditional opera reduced to potpourri; and the form of the Wagnerian music drama, again unified in itself, but no longer based on the "architectonic" principle of "absolute" music. "Especially from the purely musical perspective, one sees that, with regard to the great architectonic forms, opera in the traditional style is a very incomplete, incoherent artifice. Wagner's aspiration is not at all limited to the subordination of musical expression to the dramatic poet's artistic intentions; instead, it involves emancipating the musical art that participates in the complete art work from the chains of a defunct taste long since overcome by instrumental music, and the free development of a more unified musical form. That this form will be completely different from the traditional forms of absolute music that developed from their origins in the dance, lies in the nature of the thing."[47] Limiting the term "absolute music" to the "architectonic" form of instrumental music is justified in Hostinsky's theory of two "pure styles" (and corresponds to Wagner's and Hanslick's employment of the terms, if one limits onself to the rhetorical façades of their treatises). But just where Hostinsky arrives at a meaningful insight, there is a break in the esthetic system. The recognition that the musical form in Wagner's music dramas is *neither* exclusively founded on poetic-dramatic principles *nor* "architectonically" disposed (despite what Alfred Lorenz still believed in the 1920s) frustrates the theory of the two "pure styles" in which music comparable to sculpture and painting and "absolute", "architectonic" music form a simple dichotomy. For, although Wagner's musical form is not purely "architectonic," it cannot be completely traced back to poetic-dramatic principles; it is—at least partially—"absolute." Then again, just as with Wagner himself, the idea of absolute music that operates latently in Hostinsky's argument does not penetrate to the surface of his terminology. The words "absolute music" remain anemic.

In the battle between "formalists" and "estheticians of content" sparked by Hanslick's ideas, "pure, absolute music" was praised by the one party as the "true music," while the other either declared it a lower stage of development and a peripheral domain or denigrated it as an esthetic mistake for one of two reasons: to some the thing itself was flawed, to others the problem lay in the opinions generally held about it. Hermann Kretzschmar writes in his "Ideas for the Promotion of Musical Hermeneutics" (1902): "The view that music has only musical effect must be eliminated, and pleasure in 'absolute music' must be recognized as an esthetic obscurity. In the sense of an entirely musical content, there is no such thing as an absolute music . . . It is as much an absurdity as absolute poetry, i.e., a metered, rhyming poetry without ideas would be."[48] (It remains unclear whether Kretzschmar meant by "absolute poetry" the poetry of Stéphane Mallarmé, i.e., was combatting a phenomenon that existed in his esthetic consciousness, or whether he simply meant to demonstrate the absurdity of absolute music by comparing it to a mere figment that, due to his literary ignorance, he considered to be impossible and unreal in nature.)[49]

Strikingly, even the estheticians of content accepted Hanslick's risky distinction between "musical" and "extra-musical" forces[50] instead of reverting to the older esthetic paradigm that had preceded the romantic metaphysics of instrumental music, i.e., that "music" incorporated *logos* as well as *harmonia* and *rhythmos*. Without their perceiving it, the position they in fact still held had already been yielded terminologically. Whoever considers the text of a song or an opera to be "extramusical" has appropriated Hanslick's central thesis, whether willingly or unwillingly.

The idea of an "absolute" music that is not "architectonic" was apparent in Hostinsky without being expressed in unmistakable fashion; it was expounded in an emphatic, challenging formulation in Ferruccio Busoni's *Sketch of a New Aesthetic of Music* of 1906, which gave the term "absolute music" a new coloration. "Absolute music! What the lawgivers mean by this, is perhaps remotest of all from the absolute in music."[51] According to Busoni, music that the colloquial esthetic calls "absolute" does not deserve the name, a name aimed at the "physical manifestation" of the "absolute" in a "detached" and unfettered music. "This sort of music" — colloquially called "absolute" — "ought rather to be called 'architectonic' or 'symmetric' or 'sectional.' "[52] Busoni proclaims a "free" music, dissolved from the received forms and thus "absolute." "Such a yearning for liberation filled Beethoven, the romantic revolutionary . . . He did not quite reach absolute music, but in certain moments he divined it, as in the introduction to the fugue of the *Hammerklavier* Sonata. Indeed, all composers have drawn nearest the true nature of music in the preparatory and intermediary passages (preludes and transitions), where they felt at liberty to disregard symmetric proportions, and unconsciously drew free breath."[53] The concept of absolute music, as Busoni imagined it, reminds one of Arnold Schoenberg's idea of "musical prose." (Schoenberg's illustrations of antecedents of such "prose" were likewise "preparatory and intermediary passages" from classical works.)[54] Busoni thus imbues the concept of the "absolute in music" with the pathos of emancipation; but the dissolution expressed by the term leaves behind, as a broken shell, the very thing that determines the nature of "absolute music" in the colloquial terminology: "architectonic" form.

Busoni (similar to Debussy) saw the traditionally-based musical forms as mere boxes from which he was trying to escape. In 1913, i.e., almost contemporaneously, August Halm, who viewed the idea of musical form in ontological rather than historical terms, and saw the stamp of tradition as a prop rather than a hindrance, raised that idea to the level of the sublime. Both the elevation of "form" and its denigration occurred in the name of "absolute music." Hanslick's thesis, that the form was the spirit and the spirit was the form, recurred in an extreme version in Halm. He appropriated the objection of the "content-estheticians," that "formalism" clung to the "merely technical" and ignored the "spirit," by making a travesty of their polemics in his apologia with a provocative claim: that the "merely technical" *was* the spirit. "I admit from the start that my intention is to demonstrate that here too"—in Beethoven's Sonata in D minor, Op. 31, no. 2—"the musical, the technical, the artistic aspect is the more interesting, because it is the substantive, the intrinsic one."[55] "Of course, one says [of Beethoven] that in his sonatas and symphonies he saw not only music 'but more,' i.e., that he saw other things besides . . . Shall we let ourselves be led by Beethoven's music-philosophical lack of clarity rather than by his musical clarity?"[56]

Whereas Halm's 1913 treatise *On the Two Cultures of Music* continued the the Hanslickian rigor that excluded metaphysical digressions from the esthetics of the "specifically musical," his Bruckner book combined the emphatic concept of form with excursions into metaphysical and even religious realms—similar to Hanslick's first, "uncleansed" edition of *The Beautiful in Music*.

Halm says that the "spirit of music itself"[57] is present in "loyalty to form,"[58] a spirit that is less the subjective spirit of the composer than an objective one "that commands the composer."[59] In the "life of the form" a "spiritual law" proclaims itself.[60] And by being absolute music, music fulfilling the "law of form" instead of depicting extramusical content, instrumental music is exalted above itself to religious significance. With an excess that he himself would mistrust a decade later,[61] Halm uses Bruckner's dedication for the Ninth Symphony ("to dear God") to derive a religious interpretation of Bruckner's entire symphonic oeuvre: "A new religion of art is being created, and Bruckner's entire symphonic oeuvre served this creation, so that that dedication ought to be inscribed above all of Bruckner's symphonies, and not above one, or individual ones."[62]

Halm, it seems, avoided the term "absolute music." Only in a book on Bruckner by Ernst Kurth, whose esthetic principles are an extension of Halm's, does the double meaning of "absolute" come to characterize, in the tradition of romantic metaphysics, a musically autonomous and absolute symphonic style as being an expression of the "absolute" specifically as a result of its being "detached." Kurth distinguishes the emphatic-dialectic use of the word from the prosaic one to which Hanslick was inclined. "Either the assumption prevails that [absolute music] is simply music detached from song, sounding itself made autonomous of singing, which obviously underlay the choice of the word 'absolute,' i. e., dissolved; or, on the other hand, it is assumed that, in some manner there exists an absolute, beyond human song and human soul, for which that soul might grope, and that might suffuse the soul in the avenues of sound, united with the paths of a metaphysical event."[63] "Hence we can see clearly that the word 'absolute' has a double meaning. In a technical sense, it means dissolved from song; in a spiritual sense, dissolved from man."[64] This double meaning inspired Kurth to reinterpret Halm's thesis that Bach and Beethoven represented two opposing "cultures of music," whose synthesis in a "third culture" was contributed by Bruckner. According to Kurth, Beethoven's music is "more absolute in the technical sense"; whereas "in the spiritual sense" the "striving to dissolution from the personal" is more pronounced in Bach. "In Bruckner, music"—also as technically "absolute" music—"experiences the greatest dissolution into pure cosmic forces that had been allotted it since Bach."[65]

Wagner's esthetic façade of a primarily dramatic "total work of art" obscured his awareness of an "absolute music" that formed the substance of music drama in the form of "orchestral melody." On the other hand, the implied theory of the end of the symphony was never explicitly contradicted. Nonetheless, Kurth, though his musical feelings and thoughts were in the spirit of Wagner and Schopenhauer, did not shrink from basing an apologia for Bruckner on the historic-philosophical assertion that in Wagner, "music combined with song strove toward absolute music similarly to the way that, once upon a time, the vocal church music of the Netherlandish or Roman styles already invisibly carried within itself the longing for absolute music, and even its laws."[66] The design of this historical-philosophical construction is of romantic origin. E. T. A. Hoffmann intuited that the same spirit of the modern Christian age was revealed musically in Palestrina's vocal polyphony and Beethoven's symphonies, and thus gave historical-philosophical depth to the romantic metaphysics of instrumental music. And if Kurth claimed to see a similar relationship between Wagner and Bruckner, this means nothing less than that, under the sign of the "art religion" already conjured up by Halm, music drama and symphony, seen as different expressions of the same idea, flow into one another.

3

A Hermeneutic Model

E. T. A. Hoffmann's 1810 review of Beethoven's Fifth Symphony, a review whose introduction is one of the charters of romantic music esthetics, interprets the difference between absolute music and programmatic or "characteristic" instrumental music (which represents "determinate feelings") as the contrast between two esthetic ideas, the idea of the actually "musical" and that of the "plastic." This antithesis may at first seem to be a terminological blunder (for the process of telling a story in a piece of instrumental music does not immediately remind one of the art of sculpture), but under closer analysis it proves to be part of an overarching esthetic-historical-philosophical system capable of supporting its individual arguments even when they themselves begin to falter. "How little they recognized the true nature of music, those composers who attempted to represent such determinate feelings or even events and thus treat plastically the art form that is quite the antithesis of sculpture."[1] The historical-philosophical context that provides the contrast between "plastic" and "musical" meaning and color, a context prefigured in the works of August Wilhelm Schlegel and Jean Paul, was assumed implicitly by Hoffmann in 1810, and not presented explicitly until 1814 in the essay "Old and New Church Music"; "In the realm of art, the two opposing poles of antiquity and modernity, or of heathendom and Christianity, are sculpture and music. Christianity destroyed the one and created the other."[2] The ancient concept of God was realized in the statue, the Christian one symbolized in music, which allows one to experience the "infinite" both in vocal polyphony and in instrumental music. Esthetic and historical-philosophical categories thus overlap in Hoffmann, similarly to the way they do in Schiller's treatise "On Naive and Sentimental Poetry" or Friedrich Schlegel's essay "On the Study of Greek Poetry." The system of the arts prefigures the history of art.

The reconstruction of the system of categories to which Hoffman's antithesis "plastic-musical" belongs is intended as an attempt to express consciously a hermeneutic model to which romantic music esthetics oriented itself at almost every step, whether explicitly or implicitly. Without knowledge of this model, many of the combinations of terms Hoffmann employs as though they were obvious must strike the reader as unmotivated and arbitrary. Dichotomies such as "ancient-modern," "heathen-Christian," "natural-supernatural," "natural-artificial," "plastic-musical," "rhythm-harmony," "melody-harmony," or, finally, "vocal music-instrumental music" combine into a system that, while never appearing as such, steers the arguments from the background, as it were. Hoffmann's concatenation of antitheses is doubtless a logically questionable enterprise. Put bluntly, the process consists of nothing but the association of a pair of quite obvious opposites with other similar pairs in such proximity that finally each category on one side ("ancient," "heathen," "natural," "plastic," "rhythm," "melody," "vocal music") simply melds together with the others and may be brought into contrast with all the categories on the other side ("modern," "Christian," "supernatural," "artificial," "musical," "harmony," "instrumental music"). Obviously, logical ruptures sometimes result from this scheme of analogies and antitheses—e.g., the claim that "narrative" instrumental music is "plastic" because it is not "intrinsically" musical; but this should not obscure the profound historical meaning of the hermeneutic model, a model that belongs to the central assumptions of the romantic metaphysics of instrumental music. As we shall show, the "Querelle des anciens et des modernes," the debate over the preeminence of ancient or modern art, belongs to the antecedents of the idea of absolute music.

Hoffmann, in his Beethoven review, not only combined the antithesis "plastic-musical" with the difference between the genres of vocal and instrumental music, but also with the difference between a music that depicts certain, well-defined affections and one that is the expression of an indefinite, "endless longing." "Beethoven's music presses the levers of terror, of fear, of dread, of pain, and awakens the endless longing that is the nature of romanticism. Beethoven is a purely romantic composer (and precisely because of that, a truly musical one), which may explain why he is less successful with vocal music, which does not permit indefinite longing, but only those affections in the realm of the infinite that may be expressed in words, and why his instrumental music rarely appeals to the many."[3] The style that characterizes Beethoven's great instrumental music is, as Hoffmann's choice of words implies, the "sublime" rather than the "beautiful"; and Hoffmann alludes to the idea of associating "classical" music with the esthetic idea of the beautiful, and, in contrast, "romantic" music with the sublime, without ever expressing it in unmistakable terms.

Reviewing a symphony by Carl Anton Philipp Braun, Hoffmann describes instrumental music that allows the intimation of the "supernatural" instead of being at home in the "natural" as being primarily a "harmonic" rather than a "melodic" art. (His concept of harmony includes polyphony.) "The composer must now"—in the symphony—"demand the freedom to employ any possible means offered by the art of harmony and the endless variety of the instruments in all their combinations, and so allow the wonderful, mysterious enchantment of music to affect the listener powerfully . . . Whereas the reviewer may praise the composer of the first of the present works for having written melodiously and correctly, these higher demands are not fulfilled in the slightest."[4] That "harmony" (or polyphony) and not "melody" is the mark of the "modern, Christian, romantic" age in music is a central thesis of the essay "Old and New Church Music." Regarding Palestrina: "Without any decoration or melodic verve, chords, mostly in root position and consonant, follow one another, gripping the heart with their strength and daring, and elevating it unto the highest. Love, the consonance of all that is spiritual in nature, as it was endowed to the Christian, expresses itself in the chord, which therefore first awakened to life in Christendom; and thus the chord, harmony, becomes the image and expression of the communion of souls, of union with the eternal, of the ideal that rules over us and yet includes us."[5]

The system of esthetic-historical-philosophical analogies that Hoffmann wove about himself resulted in a seemingly insoluble problem that, in its insolubility, formed the hidden center about which the essay "Old and New Church Music" revolved: namely, how could both Palestrina's vocal polyphony and Beethoven's symphonies be considered to be the "true" or "intrinsic" music of the "modern, Christian, romantic age"? On the one hand, Hoffmann considers the "holy inspiration" that graced classical vocal polyphony to have "vanished forever from the earth" in these "impoverished times." On the other hand, modern instrumental music is not a document of decay, but a sign and a result of the irresistible "progress" of a "ruling spirit."[6] "The wondrous striving to know our heavenly home, a striving revealed in science, the force of the life-giving nature spirit, our life within that spirit, was suggested by the prescient tones of music, which spoke ever more abundantly and completely of the wonders of the distant Kingdom. For recent instrumental music has certainly elevated itself to heights the old masters could not have imagined, just as today's musicians far surpass those of the past in technique."[7] Modern instrumental music ought to be heard with "devotion," hardly different from the old vocal polyphony, as Wackenroder had already demanded. But Hoffmann associates instrumental music, which, like vocal polyphony, is primarily "harmonically" determined, with the concept of "science." Harmony, in which Jean-Philippe Rameau claimed to see the true nature of music (in contrast to Jean-Jacques Rousseau and his apologia for melody), appears both cloaked in an aura of a romantic Pythagoreanism—as a "science" that feels itself drawn to the "miraculous" instead of being adversely disposed to it—and associated with the idea of instrumental music.

The antitheses Hoffmann used were partially prefigured in the seventeenth century's theory of musical style—in the debate lover the *prima* and *seconda prattica*, which can be construed as a music-esthetic "Querelle des anciens et des modernes." Monody around 1600, like Gluck's operatic reforms or Wagner's conception of the musical drama in later times, was a return to the "ancient truth." The party of the *antiqui*, emulating Greek models, was represented by Monteverdi and the composers of the Florentine camerata, while the *moderni*, who clung to the superiority of modern times, i. e., of counterpoint, were represented by the adherents of Palestrina. The terminology is confusing: in this musical "Querelle des anciens et des modernes," the *prima prattica* is the cause of the *moderni*, the *seconda prattica* that of the *antiqui*. Vocal polyphony, however, was primarily a style of church music, and monody one of the drama and the madrigal, the literary genres that tended toward heathen or arcadian subjects. The association of the terms thus formed a tight web, almost a historical-philosophical system: the "modern," Christian age is documented in the *prima prattica*, the counterpoint of Palestrina, whereas the *seconda prattica* created a mo-nodic style in imitation of antiquity (an antiquity more imaginary than real), a style that seemed adequate for heathen-pastoral poetry. Finally, the representation of the "passions" that was the goal of the new genres, the musical drama and the monodic madrigal, stood in contrast to the "devotion" the listener was supposed to apply to vocal polyphony.

The chain of antitheses forged in the debate over *prima* and *seconda prattica* was extended by several links in the music esthetics of the eighteenth century, links in which characteristic controversies of the age hardened into slogans. New sets of contrasting concepts were combined with the received ones, though the problems that received pointed expression in these antitheses might have had little or nothing to do with the problems of the time around 1600.

Abbé Dubos's thesis, later appropriated by Rousseau and Herder, that the origin of music lay in language and that music could attain its purpose only by imitating and stylizing passionate speech, was countered in the eighteenth century by traditionalist theorists who would not be separated from the Pythagorean-Platonic idea that music rested essentially on numerical relationships. It was easy for the thesis of the origin of music in speech to associate itself with the maxims of the priority of monody—or of melody. On the other hand, the association of Pythagore-anism—the idea of the origin of music in simple propor-tions—with the accentuation of harmony was, in the music-esthetic context of the eighteenth century, a precar-ious one, although "harmony" and "proportion" had represented complementary concepts since time immemo-rial. This is because, in the older view, "harmony"—as the epitome of rationally regulated tonal relationships—was, along with rhythm, a component of "melody": to contrast the terms would have been impossible. But if, following Rameau, one moved from a mathematical justification of harmony—a Pythagorean-Platonic view of numbers as "active principles" (not as mere measurements)—to a physical foundation (the claim that the "harmony" of the major triad is prefigured in the phenomenon of the overtone series), the concept of harmony merged involuntarily with that of the chord; and the chord may be conceived as the opposite of melody (simultaneous as opposed to horizontal), or as the root of melody (broken chords with passing tones). The opposition of "harmony" and "melody"—the controversy between Rameau and Rousseau—is tied to music-theoretical premises of the eighteenth century that were not stated until "physicalism" had replaced "Platonism."

On the other hand, the concept of harmony in the eighteenth century included polyphony as well as chordal writing. And thus the concept was endowed with associations derived from the esthetics of the *prima prattica*. The amalgamation of "harmony," "polyphony," "origin of music in proportions," "church music," and "devotion"—as opposed to "melody," "monody," "origin of music in speech," "opera," and "affection"—also influenced the reception of Palestrina's music in the eighteenth and early nineteenth centuries: one tended to hear polyphonic writing chordally, or to choose works that allowed themselves to be heard chordally. As Richard Wagner put it in 1849, Christianity expressed itself musically as "harmony," as "seraphic" chordal writing.

The debate between Rousseau and Rameau over the priority of melody or harmony can, as mentioned, be seen as a music-esthetic "Querelle des anciens et des modernes." Antiquity, argued Rousseau, on the one hand knew no harmony (i.e., polyphony), and on the other produced melody with an ethos and pathos that were never again attained, let alone surpassed, by any subsequent musical culture; thus it was obvious that the transition from monody to polyphony had ruined music. "It is very difficult not to suspect that all our harmony is but a Gothic and barbarous invention."[8] ("Gothic" counterpoint is, by analogy, the musical symbol of the fall of Rome.) "M. Rameau, however, pretends that harmony is the source of the greatest beauties in music; but this opinion has been contradicted by facts and reason. By facts, because all the great effects of music have ceased, and it has lost all its energy and force since the invention of counterpoint; to which I add, that purely harmonic beauties are ingenious beauties, which please only persons versed in the art . . . By reason: because harmony furnishes no imitation by which the music, forming images, or expressing sentiments, may be raised to the dramatic or imitative genus, which is the most noble part of art, and the only energetic one."[9] Rousseau distinguishes between "imitative" music, which "expresses sentiments" or "forms images," and "natural" music, which is nothing but music, which to Rousseau is empty noise. (That Rousseau, of all people, would use the word "natural" in a pejorative sense is surprising and can only be explained by the association of "harmony" with the "natural" overtone series; however, this terminological mistake had no consequences, as "natural" was commonly given the opposite meaning in the eighteenth century, being applied to "imitative" music that depicted either external or internal nature—either the environment or the stirrings of the human soul.) "One might, and perhaps ought, to divide music into natural and imitative kinds. The first, confined only to the physics of the sounds and acting only on the senses, cannot carry its impressions to the heart, and gives sensations only more or less agreeable. Such is the music of songs, hymns, canticles, and all airs that are merely combinations of melodious sounds, and all music in general which is not harmonious. The second, using lively, accented, and, as it were, speaking inflections, expresses all the passions, paints every picture, renders every object, submits the whole of nature to its ingenious imitations, and by this means conveys to the human heart those sentiments proper for moving it."[10] Expressed anachronistically, Rousseau's "natural" music, which neither "paints" nor "moves," is "absolute" music, which he places in the shadow and views as a deficient type of "true," i.e., representative music. The dominance of the principle of imitation is unbroken as yet.

Within Rousseau's music esthetics there flow together a sentimentality that desires to be moved by music, a rationalism that demands programs (i.e., musical "painting") in instrumental music, and a longing for antiquity that opposes the modern, confused, "learned" polyphony with the soul-moving simplicity of Greek monody. Only "melody" and not "harmony" has the power to move: "If music paints only by melody, and draws from it all its force, it follows that any music that does not sing, however harmonious it might be, is not imitative; and not being able either to touch or to paint with its beautiful concords, it soon fatigues the ear, and leaves the heart cold."[11] To Rousseau, the partisan of the "anciens," "melody" is the ancient ideal that the opera of the present should strive to imitate. As "harmony," the opposing concept, is a category defined primarily in negative terms—a dark foil from which the idea of melody can be seen in relief—it encompasses heterogeneous components: instrumental music, which is empty noise as long as it does not "paint," and Palestrina's vocal polyphony, which receives the verdict of "Gothic and barbarous." The archaizing, melodic, monodic, simple, imitative music whose case Rousseau pleads is thus opposed by the "Gothic," harmonic, polyphonic, "learned," "natural" ("absolute") music tending toward "empty noise," which he disparages. Vocal polyphony and instrumental music are united within the concept of "harmonic" music, although it seems as though all they have in common is the contrast to Rousseau's idea of melody.

Rousseau, who did not let himself be influenced by the success of Stamitz's symphonies in Paris, dismissed as "plunder" any instrumental music that did not "paint." Moreover, justifications of the despised genre, such as Johann Adam Hiller attempted in 1755, remained dependent on the esthetics of sentiment, which was a theory of

vocal music, insofar as they did not dispute its premises but
merely some of its consequences: Hiller maintained that
instrumental music, too, was capable of elevating itself to a
"moving" genre. That Hiller speaks of the "wondrous"
aspect of instrumental music as well might seem disconcerting. But the "wondrous"—which he would limit, but not
exclude—is none other than instrumental virtuosity, which
causes astonishment and wonder, but which, as Quantz put
it, "does not move one especially." "Just as with other
pieces of music, nature designs the plan of concertos and
solos. It too is a song that endeavors to express artfully the
sentiments of the heart. But the wondrous should not be
excluded from it. One should apply well-chosen leaps, runs,
arpeggios, etc. in the proper places and in appropriate
measure."[12] Sentimental and rationalistic estheticians, who
sought "emotion" and "painting," misused the concept of
the "wondrous," a central category of baroque poetics, to
mean the showcasing of virtuosity in instrumental music.
(The term, which derived from a despised past, was applied
to a despised genre.) But around 1780, the "wondrous"
came into honor within music esthetics: the theory of
instrumental music received the "neobaroque" poetics of
Bodmer and Klopstock. The conviction spread that a sense
of the sublime and wonderful, and not mere naturalness
and reason, distinguished the true poet. Simultaneously,
one discovered esthetic qualities in the symphony, rather
than seeing in mere instrumental virtuosity the only
alternative to that which "painted" and "moved"; esthetic
qualities that caused one to revert to the emphatic concept
of the "wondrous" as though restoring it to its rightful
place. The "indeterminacy" of instrumental music was no
longer perceived as "empty," but rather as "sublime."

"The symphony," wrote Johann Abraham Peter Schulz
in Sulzer's *General Theory of the Fine Arts*, "is especially
appropriate for the expression of the grand, the solemn, the
sublime." The allegro of a symphony was comparable to "a
Pindaric ode in poetry. Like such an ode, it elevates and

moves the soul of the listener and demands the same spirit, the same power of imagination and knowledge of art, in order to achieve satisfaction."[13] And Carl Philipp Emanuel Bach was praised in the *Allgemeine Musikalische Zeitung* of 1801 as having been "another Klopstock" who "used tones instead of words." "Is it the poet's fault if the lyric strains of the ode he wrote appear as nonsense to the mob?" Further, Bach "demonstrated that pure music was not merely a shell for applied music, or abstracted from it, but rather . . . had the power to exalt itself to poetry, which would be that much the purer, the less the words (which always contain subordinate ideas) dragged it down to the region of the common senses."[14]

Romanticism, which took the praise of the symphony in the neobaroque spirit of Klopstock's poetics to extremes, perverted Rousseau's music esthetics into its opposite: what Rousseau had exalted was devalued, and what he had devalued was exalted. The structure of a chain of antitheses, which derived from the "Querelle des anciens et des modernes," remained intact.

It would, however, be incorrect to speak of a "romantic" music esthetics that was the esthetic of all the "romantics." August Wilhelm Schlegel, who based the music-esthetic essays in his "Lectures on Fine Arts and Literature" of 1801 on Rousseau on the one hand, and on the discussions of literary esthetics of the 1790's (Schiller's treatise "On Naive and Sentimental Poetry" and Friedrich Schlegel's essay "On the Study of Greek Poetics") on the other, avoided taking the side of "romanticism" and "modernity" in the "Querelle des anciens et des modernes": "Following our general view of the relationship between old and newer art, in music, too, we shall avoid denigrating one as opposed to the other, and rather attempt to understand the meaning of the difference."[15] Like Rousseau, but without Rousseau's value judgments, Schlegel associated the thesis of the preeminence of ancient music with the esthetic maxim that music must be the expression of "affections and movements of temperament," and with the historical claim that the origin of music, which determined its nature, was to be sought in the "natural inflections" of speech. Thus, he associated the opposite idea, that of the superiority of modern music, with the esthetic tenet that music is essentially grounded in the "harmonic relationships of tones," in proportions that manifest themselves purely and in uncompromised form in instrumental music; and finally with the historical-philosophical argument that the nature of music was not dependent on its historical origins in song, but would be discovered scientifically through the analysis of the musical art that had developed.[16]

Whereas Rousseau had designated "harmonic," "instrumental" music as *musique naturelle* (as opposed to *musique imitative*), Schlegel considered the difference between the "natural creation" (of art) in antiquity and the "artificial creation" of the modern age to be fundamental, as had been developed in the literary discussions of the 1790s. Thus the epithet "natural" migrated from modern to ancient music. Schlegel juxtaposed the "scientifically artificial development" of modern polyphony and the "natural principle" of ancient monody.[17] However, to associate modernity with artificiality and distinguish it from the principle of imitation is a reversion to baroque poetics similar to the rehabilitation of the "wondrous," which is likewise to be contrasted with the "natural." "The dichotomy of natural and artificial creation . . . points back to the French *Querelle* insofar as Perrault had based the principle of *inventio* on the planned artificiality of technical progress and had placed it above the *imitatio naturae*, i.e., the achievements of ancient art that had merely imitated nature or completed its task."[18]

Schlegel chose "rhythm," not "melody," as the ancient principle to be opposed to the modern "harmony": "If, in viewing these principal components of music, we compare the older and newer ones, we find that in the former it is the rhythmic component, in the latter the harmonic component which is more complicated by far and dominates the whole."[19] In the harmony of "newer" music, the experience of a "mystic moment" seems to be expressed: "Harmony would thus be the truly mystical principle in music, which does not build its claim to powerful effect on the passage of time, but seeks infinity in an indivisible instant."[20] Schlegel's association of antique, "purely classical, stricty delineating" art with "plasticity," and correspondingly of the modern, "romantic" art that strove for infinity with "picturesqueness" derived not from Rousseau but from the esthetic-historical-philosophical system of romanticism.[21] (In Hegel's system, painting, along with music, is characteristic of the "romantic," Christian epoch.) However, as Novalis's fragments show, the antithesis "plastic-picturesque" could be completed or even replaced by the antithesis "plastic-musical" if—unlike Schlegel, who was of a conciliatory nature—one took sides in the "Querelle" and acknowledged that modern, Christian music was the "true music" and that, conversely, music was the "true" art of the modern, Christian epoch. (In Novalis, the contrast "plastic-musical" appears as an "obvious" premise of several convoluted dialectic constructions without being presented as such.)[22]

The idea that, among the arts, music represents the "romantic" age (i.e., the medieval and modern periods) can be understood as an integration of Wackenroder's and Tieck's emphatically formulated metaphysics of instrumental music into the system of categories of the "Querelle." In a sudden reversal of esthetic judgment, "harmonic," "artificial" music, music dissolved from language and even from the expression of affections (i.e., the absolute instrumental music despised by Rousseau) had appeared as the "true" music; "indeterminacy" of content was no longer judged a deficiency but rather a hallmark of the "sublime" style, and distancing from the simple "language of the heart" was perceived as an intimation of the "infinite" rather than as a flight into empty abstraction. These

were all the motives that a partisan of modernity needed to conclude, from Wackenroder's intuition of an absolute music as related to the terminological design of the
"Querelle," that in great instrumental music the soul of a
Christian epoch was expressing itself, an epoch characterized by music, and not by plastic art. In absolute music,
music comes to itself, and the spirit it discovers as its true
nature is that of Christianity.

In the context of E. T. A. Hoffman's music esthetic, the
idea of absolute music received a formulation that gave it
historical potency. The supporting concepts of this esthetic
originated, as has been shown, in the metaphysics of
instrumental music, stated intuitively by Wackenroder and
formulated most decisively by Tieck; and also in the
musical "Querelle des anciens et des modernes," in which a
music-theoretical controversy with features that reached
back to the late sixteenth century combined with influences
from the discussions of literary esthetics of the seventeenth
and eighteenth centuries. Music esthetics—the verbal
expression of musical phenomena and problems—is hardly
less dependent on the development of literary esthetics than
on changes in music itself; and insofar as the language used
to discuss music directly affects the music as it represents
itself in the listener's consciousness, the esthetics of
literature, on whose categories and formulae the esthetics
of music feeds, belongs to the determining factors of a
history of music that does not exhaust itself in the history of
musical technique.

Hoffmann's music esthetics was partially prefigured in
the poetics of Jean Paul, a poetic theory that thereby
formed a specifically literary source of romantic music
esthetics alongside Wackenroder's originally music-esthetic
theory of instrumental music and the "interdisciplinary"
"Querelle des anciens et des modernes." Central motives of
Hoffmann's characterization of Beethoven—the emphatically historical-philosophical use of the word "romanticism," the conjuring of a "spirit world," the loss of self in

"infinite longing," the withdrawal into an "inner world," and the accentuation of "fear" and "pain"—are borrowed almost verbatim from Jean Paul's description of the "newer poetry": "The origin and character of the whole newer poetry can so easily be derived from Christianity that one might just as well call romantic poetry Christian. Christianity, like a judgment day, destroyed the whole sensual world with all its charms, crushed it into a burial mound, and put a new spirit world in its place . . . What is left to the poetic spirit after this collapse of the external world? That into which it collapsed, the internal. The mind entered itself and its night and saw spirits . . . Thus the realm of the infinite flowered in poetry over the funeral pyre of the finite . . . instead of the Greek serene joy there appeared either endless longing or unspeakable bliss . . . In the vast night of the infinite, man was more fearful than hopeful."[23]

The basic system of categories that underlies E. T. A. Hoffmann's theory of instrumental music and Jean Paul's characterization of the "newer poetry" appears in Schelling's *Philosophy of Art* of 1802, expressed as a music esthetics in the spirit of the philosophy of identity. Without being forced to lose oneself pointing into the labyrinth of speculation, one may recognize in Schelling's comparison of ancient and modern music the antitheses of the "Querelle," in which music-esthetical motives are amalgamated with those from the philosophy of history and religion. The chain of dichotomies stretches from "ancient-modern" and "state-church" across "finite-infinite" and "affection-longing" to "rhythm-harmony." "Rhythmic music, which represents the infinite within the finite, is more expresssion of satisfaction and of sprightly affect; harmonic music more of striving and longing. Thus it was necessarily in the church, whose outlook is based on longing and the tendency of diverse elements to revert to unity, that the communal striving of each individual to view himself in the absolute as being at one with all needed to express itself in harmonic, arhythmic music. In contrast, consider an alliance, e.g., the Greek states, in which something purely general (the tribe) had formed itself completely into something specific (the state) and had become that specific thing—just as the phenomenon of the state was rhythmic, its art was necessarily rhythmic."[24]

That the hermeneutic model that gained fundamental meaning for the theory of instrumental music in Hoffmann's esthetic was an "interdisciplinary" schema that took on various colors in different contexts, in no way means that it was imposed upon musical thought "from without." More to the point, it served to "give voice" to something that would otherwise have remained mute—and thus less effective. That the "artificiality" of instrumental music was praised as a sublime style, instead of being suspected as esoteric; that one perceived the "indeterminacy" of symphonic expression not as a drawback but as a sounding symbol of "endless longing" and "intimation of the absolute"; that even the popular esthetic of the symphony admitted a "harmonic" (i.e., polyphonic) style of composition instead of incessantly demanding "melody"—in other words, that there even existed an esthetic language in which an exemplary apologia for modern instrumental music of ca. 1800 could be formulated (a neccessary task, in light of Rousseau's invective)—could be attributed in no small part to the system of categories that had developed itself in the "Querelle des anciens et des modernes."

4

The Esthetics of Feeling
and Metaphysics

On May 10, 1792, Ludwig Tieck wrote to Wilhelm Heinrich Wackenroder: "Longin says that to produce something great one needs a great and sublime soul; I would go even further and claim that comprehending the great and sublime requires something of a great spirit. How else can you explain why pleasant and sentimental things affect far more minds than the great and sublime ones do? Many people do not understand or consider the latter at all. I can far more easily listen without tears to an adagio for the glass harmonica than to a psalm of Reichart's; hearing the overture to *Hamlet* or *Axur*[1] has always brought tears to my eyes: all grandeur transports me into a sort of rage—yet it passes through many people's ears without touching the soul. Reichart's wife once told me that the merely sentimental affected her far less than the sublime, from which she could never withhold her tears."[2] Tieck's brief for the sublime, which Edmund Burke and Kant had made into a basic esthetic category in the late eighteenth century, met with Wackenroder's incomprehension, for he did not wish to sacrifice the "sentimental" category: "I am not sure why the sublime should move you to tears rather than the sentimental."[3] The difference in temperament—which prohibits straightforward identification of Tieck's esthetic with that of Wackenroder—was not without influence in the theory of instrumental music developed in *Fantasies on Art*: to put it in formulaic terms, Tieck acknowledged a metaphysics of instrumental music that fed on the esthetic of the sublime, Wackenroder an esthetic religion of sentiment with its roots in pietism. Those inclined to labels from intellectual history might speak of Tieck's *Sturm und Drang* attitude as opposed to Wackenroder's tendency toward *Empfindsamkeit*. It is more important, however, to be aware that the difference between the "sublime" and the "sentimental" remains valid on either side of the boundary separating *Empfindsamkeit* and *Sturm und Drang* from romanticism; this difference reappears again and again, in various forms, in the theory of instrumental music.

It was not by coincidence that Tieck chose an adagio (for glass harmonica, no less) as his example of sentimental instrumental music, and compared it to a symphony (or overture), which he praised as sublime. Whereas the cantabile, the instrumental aria, speaks directly to the heart, the allegro, the main movement of the symphony, is "admirably suited to the expression of grandeur, of the festive and sublime," as Johann Abraham Peter Schulz wrote in Sulzer's *General Theory of the Fine Arts*.[4] And in E. T. A. Hoffmann's review of Beethoven's Fifth Symphony, which says: "Beethoven's music presses the levers of terror, of fear, of dread, of pain, and awakens the endless longing that is the nature of romanticism. Beethoven is a purely romantic composer (and for just that reason a purely musical one),"[5] the choice of words betrays that Hoffmann, too, considered the sublime style to be the truly symphonic one. If the symphony, as Tieck put it, is the "drama" of the instruments,[6] then the dramatic type to which romantic esthetics oriented itself is the Shakespearean one, the paradigmatic expression of a sublime style that places itself above the laws of beauty of "esthetic surveyors."[7] The formula that makes Beethoven a "purely romantic composer, (and for just that reason a purely musical one)" bespeaks only that it is instrumental music that, "disdaining any aid, any admixture of another art, expresses the characteristic nature of art that is only recognizable within music itself."[8] Thus Hoffmann associated the idea of absolute music—the thesis that instrumental music was the "true" music—with the esthetic of the sublime. Music that is "dissolved" from verbal and functional constraints "sublimates" or "exalts" itself above the boundedness of the finite to an intimation of the infinite.

The fact that the first, main movement of the symphony was praised as being sublime must be understood as an apologetic countermove to the polemical claim that an allegro—as opposed to a *cantabile* adagio, imitative of vocal music and therefore moving—was nothing but a pleasant or lulling noise that, as Rousseau put it, left the heart cold. The thesis that the symphony did not approach the affections and remained "speechless" was countered by the antithesis that the symphony, as "language beyond language," was exalted above those feelings conceivable on earth. Thus the concept of the sublime, like that of the "wondrous," served to justify a phenomenon that eluded the categories of the esthetics of imitation and affection that dominated in the eighteenth century. What had been perceived as a drawback, the indeterminacy of instrumental music, was reinterpreted as an advantage.

The romantic theory of "pure, absolute music" that discovered a "language above language" in "sublime" instrumental music proceeded from the *empfindsam* music esthetics of the 1780s and 1790s, and did so in a process of transformation that contemporaries must have found nearly imperceptible; this process sometimes ran its course within a single literary text, as in works of Karl Philipp Moritz, Jean Paul, and Ludwig Tieck. "Hartknopf took his flute from his pocket, and accompanied the marvelous recitative of his studies with appropriate chords. By fantasizing, he translated the language of reason into the language of sensibilities: for that was how he used music. Often, having spoken the antecedent, he would add the consequent with his flute. As he breathed his thoughts into the tones of the flute, he breathed them out of the realm of reason and into his heart."[9] Karl Philipp Moritz's allegorical novel *Andreas Hartknopf*, the source of this characterization, was published in 1785 (dated 1786); and the language in which Moritz speaks of music is entirely the language of *Empfindsamkeit* that was common in the 1780s. It is not coincidental that Hartknopf improvises on the arcadian, melancholy flute; and the simplicity and artlessness of the melodies that move the heart are characteristic. "There was nothing artful about the matter, other than that the chosen tone had to come in at just the right spot. And then it was often a very simple cadence or intonation that produced the wonderful effect."[10] The music esthetics of *Empfindsamkeit*—as opposed to the doctrine of the affections in the baroque and the philosophy of art in the classical and romantic periods—tended towards an esthetic of music as natural sound, not as work of art.

Hartknopf's *empfindsam* mood almost imperceptibly becomes a romantic one as soon as music no longer serves as the language of the heart through which one person addresses another in order to weave a sympathetic bond; but instead a tone, unexpectedly touching the innermost regions, awakens in the soul the intimation of a distant spirit realm, toward which the soul strives with endless longing. "Everyone will have noticed at least a few times in their life that some otherwise utterly meaningless tone, heard, say, in the distance, has a quite wonderful effect on the soul if the mood is right; it is as though a thousand memories, a thousand dim ideas had awakened all at once with this tone and transported the heart into an indescribable melancholy."[11] To Wackenroder, the single tone that sounds in the distance and lets one feel all the power of music becomes a note from a horn such as Weber later composed.[12]

The *empfindsam* esthetic, which was a psychology conceived by enthusiasts, was gradually replaced in the late eighteenth century by the romantic esthetic, which discussed music in metaphysical categories. And where the sentiment sought by *Empfindsamkeit* was a communal feeling (music accounted for sympathy, a melding of souls), "endless longing" arose from loneliness: from solitary contemplation of a music that was praised as "holy."

The transition that makes the music-esthetic digression in *Andreas Hartknopf* a document of intellectual history distinguishes itself similarly a decade later in *Hesperus* by Jean Paul, who belonged to the admirers of Moritz's novels. By then it is music as art, not as a sound of nature, in whose description the *empfindsam* type of reflection is replaced by a romantic one. Jean Paul's description of the effect of a Carl Stamitz symphony in the "19. Hundsposttag" of *Hesperus* consists primarily of a progression from merely stimulating the sense of hearing in the allegro to touching the heart in the adagio. The esthetic to which Jean Paul reverts is therefore quite conventional for the moment, and, because of its characterization of the allegro as mere "harmonic phraseology," even lags behind Johann Abraham Peter Schulz, who had compared the allegro of a symphony to an "uplifting, shattering" Pindaric ode.[13] "Stamitz, following a dramatic plan of a kind that not every music master designs, gradually rose from the ears into the heart, as from the allegro into the adagio; this great composer surrounds the breast that contains a heart in ever tighter circles, until he reaches it and entwines it in rapture."[14] However, the address to Jean Paul's hero that interrupts this outpouring of the heart gives this emotional ambience a turn toward the dreamy-metaphysical. "Dear Viktor! In Man there resides a great yearning that has never been fulfilled: it has no name, seeks no physical object, but anything you might call it, or any joy, it is not . . . This great, monstrous wish raises up our spirits, but at the cost of pain: alas! we who lie here below are hurled to the heights like epileptics. But our strings and tones utter this yearning that nothing can name—the longing spirit weeps harder then, and cries out in ecstatic moans between the notes: yes, all that ye speak, that I lack."[15] The romantic esthetic of music sprang from the poetic conceit of unspeakability: music expresses what words are not even capable of stammering.[16] Furthermore, it is in novels—Moritz's *Andreas Hartknopf* and Jean Paul's *Hesperus*—that the prehistory of romantic music esthetics emerged. Paradoxically enough, the discovery that music—specifically instrumental music free of object or of concrete concept—was a language "above" language occurred "in" language itself: in literature. There is nothing that justifies the assumption that Jean Paul merely put into words an esthetic that already existed in the consciousness of educated contemporaries; instead, by formulating it, he created it in the first place. In other words: literature about music is no mere reflection of what happens in the musical practice of composition, interpretation, and reception, but rather belongs, in a certain sense, to the constituent forces of music itself. For insofar as music does not exhaust itself in the acoustical substrate that underlies it, but only takes shape through categorical ordering of what has been perceived, a change in the system of categories of reception immediately affects the substance of the thing itself. And the change in the conception of instrumental music that took place in the 1790s, the interpretation of "indeterminacy" as "sublime" rather than "vacuous," may be called a fundamental one. Astonished wonderment has become wonderment filled with intimations; the "mechanics" of instrumental music become "magic." That the content of music can be determined not at all or only vaguely no longer demotes the allegro of a symphony (relative to the "moving" cantabile) but raises it to a sublime position. However, the pathos used to praise instrumental music was inspired by literature: were it not for the poetic conceit of unspeakability, there would have been no words available for reinterpreting the musically confusing or empty into the sublime or wonderful. (Already, Johann Abraham Peter Schulz had needed the poetic experience of Klopstock's odes in order to deal at all meaningfully with his experience of the symphonies of Carl Philipp Emanuel Bach.)

In Ludwig Tieck's writings, hardly differently than in Moritz's or Jean Paul's, the difference between the "pre-romantic" esthetic on which he builds and the romantic one that is his goal extends to individual texts. According to Gustav Becking, Tieck, in his essay "Symphonies," depicts Johann Friedrich Reichardt's *Macbeth* Overture (or "Symphony")—without naming the composer—as "a true product of *Sturm und Drang*, unruly, mad with effect, possessed only of the one tendency to affect the feelings and senses immediately and without the interpolation of ennobling moments."[17] And Tieck's "poetic paraphrase" is rooted in the same spirit as the "allegorical composition" itself. As Becking puts it, Tieck "celebrates the *Sturm und Drang* and envies its opportunities for direct, immediate effect."[18] Viewing the poetic amassing of hideous images he hears in the music ("Now the eye sees a hideous monster, lying in its black cave, bound with strong chains"),[19] one feels that one has returned to Tieck's early literary period, say, to the novel *William Lovell*.

On the other hand, there is no trace of "effect-mad" attitudes in the esthetic of the symphony that precedes the depiction of the *Macbeth* overture. Indeed, the theory is completely romantic in the sense that Tieck specifically does not emphasize the immediate, aggressive—intense or softly stirring—effect of music, but rather the transport to an artificial Paradise, to E. T. A. Hoffmann's "Atlantis" or "Dschinnistan": the tones "that art has discovered in a wonderful way" form "an isolated world for itself." Vocal music might still "rest on analogies to human expression" and in that sense "always be only a limited art": as instrumental music, "art is independent and free, it prescribes itself only its own laws, it fantasizes easily and without purpose, and yet it fulfills and attains the highest purpose, follows wholly its dark urges, and expresses the most profound, the most wonderful things with its dalliances."[20] Specifically as autonomous, absolute music, dissolved from "limitations" of texts, functions, and affections, art attains metaphysical honor as an expression of the "infinite." The "true" romantic esthetic of music is a metaphysics of instrumental music.

That instrumental music was capable of taking the place left empty by the conceit of unspeakability—and which was actually reserved for religious exaltation—predicated the existence of instrumental music to which one could attach a poetically inspired metaphysics without embarrassing oneself with inappropriate dithyrambs. It seems, however, that the romantic theory of instrumental music had little to do with the music-esthetical premises that originally underlay the symphonies of Stamitz or Haydn. Haydn, according to Griesinger, spoke of "moral characters" that he tried to depict in his symphonies; of the "endless longing" and "wonders of musical art" that Wackenroder and Tieck praised, he knew nothing. But that there existed an instrumental music of great quality—and that, in contrast to the works of J. S. Bach, it was known to the public of music lovers—was sufficient for the pathos of the unspeakable, a genuinely religious pathos, to seize music in its grip, primarily instrumental, indeterminate music unencumbered by empirical, "finite" limitations because of text or function.

As Heinrich Besseler recognized, the idea that instrumental music should represent a "character," a firmly outlined ethos, can be considered the central postulate of a classical music esthetic such as hesitantly came into being around 1790.[21] Besseler referred to Christian Gottfried Körner's essay "On the Representation of Character in Music," which appeared in 1795 in Schiller's *Horen*. Körner contrasts character (ethos) and affection (pathos). "Within that which we call the soul, we distinguish between something persistent and something that is transitory, between the spirit and the movements of the spirit, between the character—ethos—and the passionate state—pathos. Is it of no consequence which of the two a musician seeks to represent?"[22] In contrast to false extremes, which Körner describes in a way suggestive of the stylistic tendencies of the Baroque on the one hand, and the *Sturm und Drang* on the other; in contrast to the *style d'une teneur* that holds "fast to one single condition" and thereby becomes "uniform, exhausted, and sluggish," and to a "chaos of tones" that "expresses an incoherent mixture of passions,"[23] classical music, which Körner's esthetic-historical-philosophical dialectic seeks to justify, appears as "unity in diversity:" unity of character in a variety of passionate states.

Ludwig Tieck, whose essay "Symphonies" appeared in his *Fantasies on Art* in 1799, four years after Körner's treatise, countered the concept of "character" as central idea of romantic music esthetics with the category of the "poetic," which dominated esthetic discussions about absolute and program music, and about artistic character and triviality in music, until Robert Schumann.

The word "poetic" in no way points to a dependency of music on poetry, instead designating a substance common to all arts that, even in Tieck and Hoffmann's concept, manifests itself most purely in music. In other words: the "poetic" is an artistic idea in which, as with a Platonic idea, individual manifestations must partake in order to be art at all. "These symphonies can represent a drama so colorful, manifold, convoluted, and beautifully developed as no poet could ever provide us; for they wrap the most mysterious things in mysterious language, they depend on no laws of probability, they need relate to no history and no characters; they remain in their purely poetic world."[24] Thus, according to Tieck, instrumental music is "purely poetic" just because it is independent of literature and neither tells a story nor depicts a character. A tendency toward program music, toward "literarization" of music, is out of the question for Tieck. Even the representation of firmly outlined characters, which Haydn saw as the symphony's raison d'être, strikes Tieck as a stricture that an "independent" and "free" instrumental music seeks to avoid.[25] For Tieck as for Schumann at a later date, "music-poetic" theory is a theory of absolute music.

(The postulated independence from "laws of probability" is an attempt, however inconspicuous, to discard a central category of Aristotelian poetics, and indicates a changed conception of the poetic: whereas Plato had measured poetry by the logic of statements that are true or false, leading to the result that "poets lie," Aristotle used the logic of modalities for support, and defined poetry as representation of the possible or probable as opposed to the real or necessary. That, in contrast, Tieck seeks the "poetic" not in a seemingly plausible fiction—in the "probability" of an invented "history"—but in a quality that manifests itself most purely in instrumental music, means no less than the sketching of a new poetological "paradigm": a changed conception of that which makes poetry poetry. Romantic poetics feeds on the idea of absolute music as much as the idea of absolute music, conversely, is nourished by poetry.)

Thus what Tieck called "poetic" was also Hoffmann's idea of the "romantic," and the "purely romantic" manifests itself in the "truly musical." Like Tieck, Hoffmann distinguishes song, "in which the accompanying poetry suggests certain affections through the words," from instrumental music, which is "purely romantic" (i.e., removed from the conditions and limitations of characters and affections): it "leads us forth out of life into the realm of the infinite."[26]

The representation of affection or character (terms that often overlap in romantic music esthetics—as opposed to Körner's—because both, instead of being considered for themselves, merely belong to the dark background that sets off the idea of the "poetic"), that is, the fixation of instrumental music on finite and bounded things that Tieck

and Hoffmann found inadequate, appears in Hans Georg
Nägeli's 1826 *Lectures on Music with Consideration of
Amateurs* as the object of a polemic whose zeal and vehe-
mence can be explained as didactic—as "consideration of
amateurs." "Whenever the word 'character' has been used
in relation to music—and that term is always taken to
mean instrumental music here—it has been misused.
Whenever one has spoken, or tried to speak, of a certain
character of a musical work, one has spoken in the most
uncertain terms; and thus one was never able to express
what was actually characteristic in a given piece of
music."[27] "Affections" and "scenes," the characteristic
and the pictorial, are banned from the "play of form" that
Nägeli conceives instrumental music to be. "It must banish
every specific affection, every mixture of affections from
the mind, must overshadow, so to speak, every coincidental
viewpoint."[28] The "characteristic" receives the same verdict as the "programmatic": it is not "poetic."

The "poeticizing" hermeneutics of romanticism, the
attempt to put in stammering words that which is beyond
words, must not be misconstrued as determination of
characters, as Hermann Kretszchmar postulated, let alone
as a sketch of "esoteric programs" in Arnold Schering's
sense. The effort to speak the unspeakable often begins
with an admission of its own hopelessness; the first sentence
already takes back those that follow. And there would be
nothing more false than to accuse an exegete such as Tieck
or Hoffmann of having a poetic sketch of the "hidden
meaning" of music: of the "text" that the tones "encode."
That one nonetheless attempted an interpretation of the
"poetic" at all—while conscious of its general insufficiency—bespeaks, on the other hand, that absolute music—understood to be the realization of the idea of a
"purely poetic" art—did not exhaust itself in being form
and structure. Formulated paradoxically, it contained a
surplus in which one sensed its nature. "But what words
should I resort to, should I grasp, in order to express the

power that heavenly music, with its full tones, its charming reminiscences, has over our heart? With its angelic presence, it enters the soul immediately and breathes heavenly breath. Oh, how all memories of all bliss fall and flow back into that one moment, how all noble feelings, all great emotions welcome the guest! Like magical seeds, how rapidly the sounds take root within us, and now there's a rushing of invisible, fiery forces, and in an instant a grove is rustling with a thousand wonderful flowers, with incomprehensibly rare colors, and our childhood and an even more distant past are playing and jesting in the leaves and the treetops. Then the flowers become excited and move among one another, color gleams upon color, lustre shines upon lustre, and all the light, the sparkling, the rain of beams, coaxes out new lustre and new beams of light."[29] Tieck's "poeticizing" sketch, a poem in prose that seeks to "grasp" the "purely poetic" substance of a piece of music, differs from a "program" or a "characterization" by the "beautiful confusion"[30] with which the metaphors change and the most divergent realms of reality cross over into one another. But it is just the arbitrariness, the unbounded imagination with which Tieck wounds prosaic logic, that turns this exegesis into a poetic text that lets the reader imagine what is granted the hearer of absolute music: an experience that overcomes him for an instant, but which cannot be held fast. The musical impression is as fleeting as it is compelling, the poetic paraphrase lingering but insufficient.

In contrast to the formalistic esthetic that draws a line between absolute music and poeticizing or programmatic intentions (instead of separating absolute, poetic music from programmatic or characteristic music), romantic esthetics understood absolute music to be the realization of the "purely poetic." And, for Tieck and later for Schumann (following Jean Paul), the opposite of the poetic was the prosaic. But music became prosaic—and the outlines of a truly "absolute" music are distinguished in the negation of the prosaic—whenever it subordinated itself to extramusical purposes that endangered its metaphysical worth, or wandered off into empty virtuosity (whether compositional or interpretative), or made itself dependent on programs that provoked petty tone painting, or wasted itself on feelings that were considered mundane. In other words: along with functionality and programmatic or characteristic intent, musically expressed sentiment came under suspicion of triviality.

What Novalis said of poetry was no less true of the music in which one found the idea of the "poetic" realized most purely: "That poetry should create no affections is clear to me. Affections are virtually something fatal, like diseases."[31] And Friedrich Schlegel, who tended to use brusque fragments to say what others timidly offered in treatises, deprecated the idea that music "is only the language of sentiment" as simply the "flat viewpoint of so-called naturalness." "Some think it strange and ludicrous when musicians speak of the thoughts in their compositions . . . But whoever has a sense of the wonderful affinities of all arts and sciences will at least refrain from considering the matter from the flat viewpoint of so-called naturalness, according to which music is only the language of sentiment; and will not consider a certain tendency of all pure instrumental music toward philosophy to be impossible of itself.[32]

That Schlegel combined his attack on rationalism (the unmistakable target of the words "flat" and "so-called naturalness") with an objection to the esthetics of feeling may come as a surprise; for the opinion that, inversely, the romantic esthetic was an esthetic of feeling and the rationalistic one was (or ought to have been) an esthetic of structure, is one of those resilient prejudices of the history of ideas that are so deep-rooted that the historian hardly stands a chance of exterminating them. But insofar as one takes the romantic music esthetic to mean the music esthetic

of the romantics, that esthetic—as metaphysics of instrumental music—is at least as far removed from the esthetics
of feeling as it is from Hanslickian formalism. (The
dichotomy that Hanslick forced upon his times is inadequate for the early nineteenth century.)

The esthetics of feeling—the association of the expressive with the simple and natural: the expectation that a
composer or interpreter expresses himself through the
music, "breathes his soul into sounds," in order to awaken
sympathy in the listeners; that, in other words, music was
a means to "create" an unconventional, "generally
human," "unalienated" sociability and communality—
can be understood sociohistorically as a bourgeois esthetic that remained nearly untouched by the progression
of the history of ideas through the Enlightenment, *Empfindsamkeit*, *Sturm und Drang*, popular romanticism,
and *Biedermeier*. It documents itself already at the beginning of the eighteenth century in the the *Critical Reflections*
of Abbé Dubos: "Just as painting imitates the forms and
colors of nature, music imitates the tones, the accents, the
sigh, the modulations of the voice, in short, all the sounds
through which nature itself expresses feelings and
passions."[33] On the other hand, the chain of citations with
which Hanslick ended the first chapter of his polemic
against the "decayed esthetic of feeling"[34] speaks to its
unbroken existence up to the middle of the nineteenth
century.

In contrast, the romantic theory of instrumental music is
a metaphysics that was developed in opposition to the
esthetics of feeling, or at least to its more popular variants.
Schlegel compares musical form to a philosophical meditation in order to make clear that form is spirit and not the
mere shell of a representation of affections or an expression
of feelings. Romanticism—the authentic kind, not trivial
romanticism—contrasted simplicity with the "beautiful
confusion" of the artistic, the natural with the wondrous,

and the sociable cult of feelings with the metaphysical intimation that a solitary person gains in musical contemplation that forgets the self and the world.

Characteristic as it is of romantic esthetics, the brusque gesture with which Novalis and Friedrich Schegel turned away and polemically distanced themselves from the bourgeois culture of feelings — in which music, as the language of sensibilities, provided sympathy and communality — nonetheless appears as an extreme manifestation of the romantic approach, which also admitted other expressions. Where Novalis, horrified by sentimental communality that could become digusting, spoke of affections as if they were diseases that might infect him, Schlegel speaks of "material filth"; but he ascribes a cathartic effect to music. "It seems to purify the passions of the material filth that clings to it, by representing the passions in our inner mind without reference to objects, but only by their form; and, having stripped them of their mundane shell, allows them to breathe the pure ether."[35]

In the nineteenth century, the idea that feelings or affections were expressed by music "only in their form" was a music-esthetic commonplace that had varying versions and changing accents. However, the same premise — the thesis that feelings described by music were non-representational and non-conceptual — permitted divergent and contradictory consequences. That music is only capable of capturing feelings in the abstract, only vaguely, as it were, did not prevent Arthur Schopenhauer from emphasizing the expression of feelings — and not musical form — as the decisive force: the object of music was the "will" (understood to be the epitome of affections), the blind drive and urge in which Schopenhauer thought he had discovered the "thing in itself" behind the appearances of the world. Thus he sees the very abstractness — instead of being a deficit — as vouching for the fact that musically expressed feelings do not cleave to the empirical manifestations of the world, but instead penetrate to its

metaphysical nature. Mediated by the force of nonrepre-
sentativeness, the eighteenth-century esthetics of feeling
receives a turn toward the metaphysical. Music "never
expresses appearances, but solely the inner nature, the
of-itself of all manifestation, the will itself." What it
expresses is "therefore not this or that individual and
specific joy, this or that grief, or pain, or dismay, or
rejoicing, or merriness, or calmness; but rather joy, grief,
pain, dismay, rejoicing, merriness, or calmness *themselves*,
in the abstract to some extent; it expresses the essential side
of these, lacking all details, and therefore also their
motives."[36] What Schopenhauer called "essential," Hanslick demoted to the "inessential." To Hanslick, the non-
representational and abstract character of musical expression means that music is restricted to expressing the
"dynamic" aspect of feelings. "Not love, but only a
movement can be expressed by it, a movement that could
occur in love or also in some other affection, but which
nonetheless is always the inessential part of its character."[37] And Hanslick's central argument, which founded
music-esthetic "formalism," states that an indeterminate, undifferentiated dynamics of feeling cannot be the
esthetic substance and raison d'être of a determined,
differentiated musical form. (Schopenhauer tried to solve
the same problem as Hanslick, namely how the nonrepre-
sentativeness of musical expression was related to the
determinacy of musical form, but came to the opposite
conclusion: "Its generality is, however, not at all the
empty generality of abstraction, but of a completely
different kind, and is connected with universal, clear
determinacy."[38] The correlation between "universal determinacy" of structure and of expression nonetheless remains
a mere assertion.)

Schopenhauer's variant of the esthetic of feeling, the
idea that, by its abstractness, a musically expressed
affection exalts itself to metaphysical honor, seems to have
been inspired by Wackenroder. Instead of a resigned,

darkened metaphysics of the "will," Wackenroder sees esthetic "devotion" under the sign of the "art religion" in whose context the thought of musical expression of feelings "in the abstract" receives philosophical meaning.

The feelings that come about in selfless esthetic contemplation—concentrating on the music, and not lost in the coincidental stirrings of one's own spirit—must be stored as firmly defined affections determined by words in order to find their way into "pure, absolute music." "When all the inner vibrations of our heartstrings—the quiverings of joy, the storms of ecstasy, the loudly beating pulses of consuming worship—when all these demolish the language of words, the tomb of the heart's inner rage, with one shout, then they emerge as though transported into the transfigured beauty of heavenly life, in the vibrations of lovely harp strings, and celebrate their resurrection as angels."[39] Instrumental music appears as the redemption of feelings from the chains of vocal, word-bound music. Only by "separating the so-called sentiments"—as Wackenroder, in a clear distancing from *Empfindsamkeit* and its social culture of feelings, says—"from the confused jumble and web of the earthly nature in which they are entangled, and executing them [as works of art] for our pleasant remembrance, and storing them in our own way,"[40] do they receive artistic meaning, which, to Wackenroder, simultaneously implies artistic-religious meaning. "Sometimes these feelings that arise in our hearts seem so magnificent and great that we enclose them like relics, in precious monstrances . . . There have been various beautiful inventions for the storage of feelings, and thus have all the fine arts come to be. But I consider music to be the most wonderful of these inventions, because it portrays human feelings in superhuman fashion."[41] Musical expression of feelings was "sacralized" by Wackenroder with unforeseeable consequences for the music esthetics of the nineteenth century. On the other hand, however, the exaltation of feelings into the immense removed them so far from their source that the distance that separates Wackenroder from *Empfindsamkeit* seems hardly smaller than the distance from an esthetics of form with a metaphysical "superstructure" such as Ernst Kurth, for instance, proclaimed in the twentieth century. However, the artistic-religious "exaltation"above the tradition of *Empfindsamkeit* was adapted by the bourgeois culture of feelings—whose *empfindsam* expression continued as an undercurrent in the classic-romantic age and found its continuation in the Biedermeier period as an edifying set-piece.

Wackenroder's esthetic of instrumental music—an esthetic in which absolute music appears as an intimation of infinity as revealed to a feeling that, dissolved from all "material filth," is in itself already religion—was translated by Karl Wilhelm Ferdinand Solger and Christian Hermann Weisse into the language of dialectic philosophy, a language that by no means dampened the emphatic claim of esthetic philosophy, in which the religion of art and the religion of feelings were pervasive, but instead intensified it insofar as a doctrine that, if necessary, could have been excused as poetry by the educated among its detractors now presented itself as a work of science.

In the chapter on music in his 1819 *Lectures on Esthetics* (published poshumously in 1828), Solger begins with Herder's intuition that "the common soul, the simple concept of the being of existing things" expresses itself in "sound itself."[42] "Music alone exists not merely for the expression of specific sentiments; these are nothing but momentary conditions that in art can be made into something by being combined into a whole. Momentary sentiment must therefore make itself heard with the simplicity of the human character." That, in other words, a unity of character must underlie a multiplicity of changing emotional stirrings if the central postulate of the esthetic, which is simultaneously one of ethics, is to be fulfilled, reminds one of Körner's sketch of a classical esthetic of music that was based on the contrast between *pathos* and *ethos*. However, the emphasis on art religion to which Solger rises is an inheritance of Romanticism. Music is "both the inner feeling of the soul itself and an expression of specific sentiment. Both aspects must express themselves profoundly and in just that way represent the idea, as music is always perceived as generality, which itself is perceived simultaneously as a momentary condition." In the language of dialectic philosophy, "idea" means the transmission of generality and specifics. However, Solger, similarly to Schleiermacher, seems to have considered the "inner feeling of the soul" to be the place where religion forms itself as uplift through lowering of the self; otherwise, the transition from "inner feeling" as self-consciousness to the perception of the "presence of the eternal" could hardly be explained. "Thus music is capable of transporting us into the presence of the eternal even by the moment of its appearance, as it dissolves our sentiment into the unity of the living idea . . . Music dissolves our own consciousness into the perception of the eternal. Accordingly, the characteristic, essential use of music is the religious one."[43] What Körner called "ethos"—the binding by which the momentary arousals of feeling expressed by music are held together—has for Solger become a religious experience transmitted by art and rooted in the "inner feeling of the soul."

In Weisse's *System of Esthetics*, published in 1830, it is absolute instrumental music that most comprehensibly characterizes and makes perceptible the "modern spirit" as it raises itself to awareness of its self-sufficiency and independence. "The vitality of the spirit that takes shape in instrumental music, a characteristic shape differentiated from all specifics that lag behind the realm of beauty,[44] expresses itself in this art form as a continual undulating or hovering between the two opposite poles of sadness and joy, or of lament and rejoicing:[45] mutual sentiments or states which appear here in their purity as attributes of the absolute, or, should one already care to use this expression here, the divine spirit, without immediate relation to that which otherwise awakens, incorporates, and accompanies it in the finite human spirit."[46] The feelings *in abstracto*, purified of "material filth," that Wackenroder wanted to "enclose like relics in precious monstrances"[47] —and absolute instrumental music was to him nothing but such a monstrance—appear in Weisse, in perhaps the most extreme possible formulation of the doctrine of art religion as religion of feelings, as "attributes of the divine spirit."

5

Esthetic Contemplation as Devotion

In the panegyric preface to his monograph *On Johann Sebastian Bach's Life, Art, and Works*, Johann Nikolaus Forkel wrote that he had "come to the opinion that one can only speak of Bach's works with rapturous joy if one knows them well; and of some of them only with a kind of holy worship."[1] The religious tone Forkel adopted (not without hesitation) was still quite unusual in 1802 in discussions of works of art. And Forkel's impression that approaching musical creations with "holy worship" did not cross the line into blasphemy must have come from his reading of Herder or Tieck and Wackenroder.

In 1793, after a "sojourn in Italy" that let him "reflect more on liturgical music than there would have been opportunity for in Germany,"[2] Herder wrote in an essay, "Cäcilia": "For devotion, I think, is the highest result of music, holy, heavenly harmony, humility, and joy. By this route, music has carried off its most beautiful treasures and attained the innermost point of art."[3] The "holy" art for which Herder requires "devotion" is the music of "a Leo, Durante, Palestrina, Marcello, Pergolesi, Handel, Bach."[4] The present impresses Herder as an "impoverished time;" but bygone grandeur, a grandeur that can be remembered even if it has vanished from reality, lets one draw hope that the path to a second era of church music is not blocked. "Holy music has no more died out than the true feeling of religion and simplicity can die out; meanwhile, of course, it awaits and hopes for a time of restoration and revelation."[5]

Thus the "holy" musical art whose idea Herder invoked in 1793 was not simply music but the "true" church music, whose principles he found realized in Bach as in Palestrina. (The narrow definition of churchly music to which the Palestrina enthusiasts of the nineteenth century, Protestant as well as Catholic, withdrew, was still foreign to Herder.) But in Herder's *Kalligone* of 1800, a metacritique of Kant's "Critique of Reason," "devotion" is "the highest result of music," a feeling that Herder brings to music as a whole, including and especially absolute music "separated from words and gestures." "You who despise the music of tones for being such and cannot gain anything from it"—he means Kant—"if you cannot get anything from it without words, then stay away from it . . . The slow process of its history demonstrates how difficult it has been for music to separate itself from its sisters, words and images, and to develop as an art for its own sake. A unique, compelling means was required to make it self-sufficient and separate it from outward assistance."[6] Herder therefore feels that the origin of music in song therefore does not exclude that its telos, in which its nature shows itself, is absolute music.

But the "compelling means" that would allow autonomous music, divorced from functions and texts, to appear meaningful at all, and to be art in the emphatic sense, was sought by Herder less in the structure of the thing than in the constitution of the listener's consciousness. In other words: according to Herder, absolute music's claim to be "conceptless beauty," existing 'purposely without purpose" for its own sake instead of supporting actions or illustrating texts, can only be justified in that the listener withdraws into a state of contemplation unaware of self or world, in which the music appears as an "isolated world for itself."[7] The legitimation of absolute music lies in esthetic contemplation and its meaning for the "education of humanity," and conversely esthetic immersion is legitimized by the expressiveness of absolute music that elevates itself above words. "What was the thing that separated it"—music—"from all things foreign, from sight, dance, gesture, even from the accompanying voice? Devotion. It is devotion that elevates humans and a gathering of humans above words and gestures, for then there is nothing left for their feelings except—tones."[8]

The claim that it would be appropriate to hear a piece of absolute music with "devotion," rather than allowing oneself to be stimulated to conversation through the pleasant yet empty sounds (which Sulzer, the incarnation of "common sense" in the late eighteenth century, still perceived instrumental music to be), was in no way taken for granted in 1800; instead, it was rather alienating. However, the transportation of "devotion" from "holy" music to absolute music was not, as a detractor of the "art religion" of the nineteenth century might impute, mere enthusiasm, but represented nothing less than the discovery, fundamental to the musical culture of the nineteenth century, that great instrumental music, in order to be comprehended as "musical logic" and "language above language," required a certain attitude of esthetic contemplation (most urgently described by Schopenhauer), an attitude through which it constituted itself in one's awareness in the first place. To use Husserl's phenomenological terminology, contemplation is noesis to the noema that is absolute music.

But Herder's insight predicated that "indeterminate" music "divorced from words and gestures" appeared as the "true" musical art, not as a deficient mode of vocal music. Only if wordless music "elevates" itself above speech, instead of remaining beneath it, can one sensibly allow elevation to religious devotion and the contemplation of absolute music to merge into one another.

It is certainly not impossible that Herder was forced to the conclusion that one must bring a feeling of "devotion" to absolute music as to "holy" music by his own experiences and by opposition to Kant, the detractor of instrumental music; but he was more likely influenced by Wackenroder. (The *Outpourings of the Heart of an Art-Loving Friar* had appeared in 1797, the *Fantasies on Art* in 1799.) And it was Wackenroder in whose language a whole century expressed the devotion to which it felt enraptured by music. "When Joseph was at a big concert, he would sit down in a corner without seeing the glittering assemblage of listeners and listen with just the same devotion as though he were in church—just as still and immobile, and with the same eyes looking at the floor in front of him. Not even the least tone escaped him, and at the end he was exhausted and tired from the intense attentiveness . . . In happy and delightful symphonies in full voice, which he loved above all, it seemed to him as though he saw a frolicking chorus of youths and maidens dancing in a pleasant meadow . . . Some places in the music seemed so clear and vivid to him that the sounds seemed to him to be words. At other times, the tones effected a wonderful mixture of happiness and sadness in his heart, so that he felt equally close to smiling and crying . . . All these manifold sentiments thus always brought forth corresponding images and new thoughts in his soul: a wonderful gift of music—which art generally affects us all the more powerfully and sets every force of our being into all the more turmoil, the darker and more mysterious is its language."[9]

For Wackenroder-Berglinger (in the cited passage, Wackenroder and Berglinger, novelist and character, are identical), the word "devotion" must be construed in an almost unmetaphorical way. The *Fantasies on Art* do refer to a "bold analogy" in which the disciples of art religion, who "kneel down before art with upright hearts and bring with them the homage of an eternal and unbounded love," are compared to one "elected to priestly ordination, who finds beautiful reasons everywhere in life to honor his God and thank him."[10] But the "analogy" crosses over into straightforward, unqualified profession of belief when Wackenroder reveres "the deeply grounded, immutable holiness belonging to this art"—music—"above all others"[11] or Tieck even fearlessly unites religion and art: "For music is certainly the ultimate mystery of faith, the mystique, the completely revealed religion."[12]

The "devotion" to which Wackenroder-Berglinger feels elevated is valid for all music, in principle, without regard to genre or level of style. "I have always experienced that whatever music I am hearing seems to be the best and most exquisite, and makes me forget all other kinds."[13] (The one "elected to priestly ordination," whom Wackenroder compares to the believer in the art religion in a "bold analogy," "builds his altar anywhere.") Yet it is the "full-voiced symphonies" that he "loved above all." And Tieck, even more forcefully than Wackenroder, states that the idea of music reveals itself most clearly in great instrumental music, what Hanslick called "pure, absolute music."[14]

The kind of listening that Wackenroder describes in "Joseph Berglinger" must seem contradictory to a reader who has grown up with the esthetic categories of the twentieth century. On the one hand, he speaks of intense concentration on the matter itself, the musical phenomenon, the topic; on the other, of "perceptible images and new ideas" suggested by the music. And both Wackenroder[15] and Tieck,[16] in their *Fantasies on Art*, describe their impressions on hearing symphonies in a language characterized by its almost rampant metaphors. Yet one misunderstands the descriptions if one reads them with the undifferentiated mistrust a "formalist" has for all kinds of "hermeneutics." It is important that, in the terminology of the time around 1800, they are neither "historical" nor "characteristic," but rather "poetic": they tell no story, and they avoid naming a specific, well-delineated pathos or ethos as whose expression the music is intended to be. Instead, they are meant to be attempts to speak of the poetic (not in the sense of "literary," but "metaphysical") nature of music in analogies that intertwine themselves into mysterious and labyrinthine figures, as though indicating that music is a "language above language." Symphonies, wrote Tieck, "reveal the most mysterious in mysterious language, they do not depend on laws of probability, they do not need to attach themselves to any story or character, they remain in their purely poetic world."[17]

It would seem as though the types of musical listening that in 1797 merge into one another in "Joseph Berglinger" were brusquely differentiated into "true" and "false" ways of enjoying music in the sketch of a theory of reception that Wackenroder wove into a 1792 letter to Tieck. "When I go to a concert, I find that I always enjoy the music in two ways. Only one form of pleasure is the true one: it consists of observing the sounds and their progression in the alertest way; in the complete dedication of the soul to this onrushing stream of sensations." (As with Kant, sensory impressions and feelings seem to merge together in the term "sensations.") "Distant and detached from any disturbing thought and from all foreign sensory impressions. This miserly gobbling-up of tones is connected with a certain exertion that one cannot endure very long . . . The other way that music delights me is not a true enjoyment of it at all, not a passive reception of the impressions of the tones, but rather a certain activity of the soul that is stimulated and sustained by music. Then I no longer hear the sentiment that prevails in the piece, but my thoughts and fantasies are abducted as if on the waves of song, and often lose themselves in distant hiding places."[18] (The term "passive" might arouse suspicion: modern esthetics tends to perceive the concentration on the work that Wackenroder calls "passive reception of the impressions of the tones" as "active listening" in Hugo Riemann's sense, as a recreation of the compositional process; and conversely, to explain losing oneself in images and thoughts that lead away from the music as being "passive" and at the mercy of "mechanical" associations.)

If one goes from the premises of an esthetic of the "specifically musical," the description in "Joseph Berglinger" appears to be a reversion into indistinctness and mongrel "hermeneutics": as a smudging of the borders drawn in Wackenroder's letter. But one must not confuse the "poetic" descriptions in *Fantasies on Art* with the flight into images and thoughts that Wackenroder used to reproach himself for "false" music listening. "Pure, absolute music" is never travestied as a "programmatic" or "characteristic " music, but always interpreted "poetically." Although the result is sometimes a regrettable clash of metaphors, the analogies remain in the sphere of an indeterminacy redeemed by intimations, in which romantic esthetics sought the metaphysical origin of instrumental music. And the relevant characteristics of contemplation, i.e., the behavior that forms a correlate to the idea of absolute music, remain intact in "Joseph Berglinger" just as they did in the sketch of "true" listening from 1792: the distancing of absolute music from programmatic and characteristic music; further, the "endless longing" that, as elevation above the captivity of words in the finite and conceptual, makes up the "poetic nature" of music; and finally, concentration on the work ntead of losing oneself in stray thoughts and feelings.

That esthetic contemplation was able to appear as devotion was the reverse of the process in which religious devotion sometimes reached the threshold of becoming esthetic contemplation. (The interlocking changes in the philosophical realms of art and religion—an interaction that manifests itself as an event in the "history of ideas," which, as Wilhelm Dilthey believed, is less a cause than an outcome—may be expressed through the formula that the "sacralization" of the profane is analogous to the "secularization" of of the sacred. And even if, as a historian without religious dogma, one would like to avoid the stigma of unjustified appropriation inherent in the word "secularization," one may still view a phenomenon such as the art religion of the nineteenth century as a historically legitimate manifestation of religious consciousness.)

In the *Lectures on Religion* that Friedrich Schleiermacher directed at the "educated among its detractors" in 1799—the year of Wackenroder and Tieck's *Fantasies on Art* and Herder's *Kalligone*—he abruptly separated religion from metaphysics or speculation on the one hand, and from morality or practice on the other. "Its nature is neither thought nor action, but rather contemplation and feeling."[19] "Praxis is art, speculation is science, religion is a sense and taste for the infinite."[20] But "contemplation and feeling"—contemplation of the finite as it stands, visible and immediate, and feeling for the infinite with which it is interwoven—are described in turns of phrase based undeniably on the model of esthetic contemplation. "Contemplation without feeling is nothing and can have neither the right source nor the right force. Feeling without contemplation is likewise nothing: both are something only when, and because, they are originally one and inseparate. That first mysterious moment that occurs in every sensory perception before contemplation and feeling have separated, when the sense and its object are as though they have flowed together and become one, before each has returned to its original place—I know how indescribable it is, yet I wish you could hold it fast and recognize it again in the higher and godly religious activity of the soul."[21]

In a theology that does not disdain to approach poetry, one must take metaphors seriously. In the lecture "On the Nature of Religion," in which Schleiermacher separates action from religion, he compares the religion that accompanies action without motivating it to "holy music": "All real actions should and can be moral, but religious feelings ought to accompany all the deeds of man like a holy music;

he should do everything with religion, but nothing because of religion."[22] Music can be "holy" because, inversely, holiness as Schleiermacher understands it is capable of manifesting itself in music. The religion that Schleiermacher preached to "the educated among its detractors" is a "religion of feelings," or, to put it negatively, not a religion of the word. It hovers around the "ineffable" rather than grasping at what has been "spoken." Creeds are merely secondary expressions of "pious states of mind" "represented in speech," and not their substance.[23] However, the "ineffable"—the objective correlative to the subjective "inner state" in which religion constitutes itself—can be enciphered through music, which is a language above language. "Of the three areas of speech, poetic, oratorical, and factually didactic, the poetic is the highest, and above them all and better than them is music."[24]

Schleiermacher represented Protestant theology of the nineteenth century. From his doctrine that propositions are truly theological propositions to the extent that they cause the religious feeling to become more sure of itself, one may without false generalization conclude that the art religion of the nineteenth century was truly a religion and not just a travesty of one. For the fact that music expresses the feeling of infinity that is the substance of religion was sufficient to allow esthetic contemplation and religious devotion to flow into one another without having Schleiermacher's theological premises—which can be seen as theological premises for the entire century—be suspected of being superstition. The theologian of feeling—feeling that was "immediate self-awareness" on the one hand and the perception of "simple dependency" on the other—was simultaneously, if implicitly, the theologian of the art religion.

The ideas that Schleiermacher hesitantly suggested were proclaimed frankly in a broadside, "The New Church," which the Berlin theologian Martin Leberecht de Wette published anonymously in 1815: "Art and poetry," he says, "are the most effective means of awakening religious feelings in the educated people of our time. Faith makes itelf known most immediately in feelings. And religious feelings are best served by art."[25]

Among the Catholic theologians, it was Johann Michael Sailer who praised art as the means of religious awakening. In a lecture at Landshut University in 1808, 'On the Alliance of Religion with Art,' he rejected "the merely esthetic religion that only floats in indeterminate feelings of holiness,"[26] but on the other hand emphasized: "Religion and art exist in an alliance that is not coincidental, not arranged, but substantial, necessary, that did not come about today or yesterday, but is eternal."[27] According to Sailer, the "one holy art" is "one of the organs that reveal the life of religion" and allow the "inner, invisible" religion to come forth as "outward, visible."[28] And the reverse: "Now if, aside from the life that goes outward, religion also has a life that returns inward, and enters deep into the affected soul, then the one holy art has a new dignity: it is not merely a tool of outward religion, but also a tool of inward religion."[29]

6

Instrumental Music and Art-Religion

The art-religion of the nineteenth century, the belief that art, though created by humans, is revelation, has fallen into disrepute as a "murky mixture." The protest against it as formulated by, say, Igor Stravinsky, directed itself against the sacralization of art on the one hand, and against the secularization of religion on the other, and is thus doubly motivated: one feels the need to protect religion from the misuse of art as much as to protect art from the misuse of religion. If, instead of being outraged at some piece of "wretched nineteenth-century excess" in the name of dialectical theology or music-esthetic formalism, one appreciates Schleiermacher's religion of feelings as a developmental phase in its own right within the history of piety and theology, then one sees that a concept of art with an impulse toward religion and a concept of religion impelled toward art met in art religion without there being a question of either one falsifying the other in transmission. The historian is in no way entitled to speak of "illegitimacy." On the other hand, the idea of art religion, before its degeneration into a formula for edification, had always been perceived as a problem, and not as a straightforward, undoubted dogma; and the complicated dialectic in which a religiously-philosophically inspired esthetic wraps itself is nowhere revealed more distinctly than in the theory, the metaphysics of instrumental music.

In his 1799 *Lectures on Religion*, Schleiermacher, who

seems to be the source of the term "art religion," distinguished three paths that allow one to go from the finite to the infinite: self-absorption, absent-minded contemplation of a piece of the world, and finally the devotional contemplation of works of art. Schleiermacher admits that viewing the infinite through esthetic contemplation is denied him personally: "I would wish, were it not sinful to wish beyond oneself, that I could observe just as clearly how artistic sensibility for itself becomes transformed into religion, how, despite the tranquility in which the spirit is immersed by every single enjoyment, it nonetheless feels driven to make the progress that can lead it to the universe. Why are those who may have gone this way such silent natures? I do not know it, that is my severest limitation, it is the gap I feel deep in my nature, but also treat with respect. I resign myself not to see, but—I believe; the possibility of the thing stands clearly before my eyes, only to be kept secret from me."[1] On the other hand, Schleiermacher believes that none of the historical religions came from the contemplation of art: "I have never heard anything of an art religion that dominated peoples and ages."[2] But he is convinced of the possibility of an art religion; and he coined the term for a thing of which he could only perceive the abstract outline, but which was simultaneously (1799) receiving the concrete form of living experience in Wackenroder and Tieck's *Fantasies on Art*, an experience that Schleiermacher intimated, though he lacked it in himself.

The dogma of the art religion was fomulated most forcefully by Tieck: "For music is certainly the ultimate mystery of faith, the mystique, the completely revealed religion. I often feel as though it were still in the process of being created, and as though its masters ought not to compare themselves with any others."[3] This quotation comes from the essay "Symphonies," whose central thesis is the claim of instrumental music's superiority to vocal music; therefore, the "music" that elevates itself to a religion would seem to mean primarily instrumental music. And the expression "still in the process of being created" may be comprehended as an intimation of the fact that Tieck's metaphysics of instrumental music, which was originally coined in response to works by Johann Friedrich Reichardt, did not find an adequate object until E. T. A. Hoffmann borrowed Tieck's language in order to do justice to Beethoven.

Tieck's art religion is an expression of the desire to lock out the world and withdraw into a contemplation whose esthetic character involuntarily merges into a religious one: "I have always yearned for this redemption, and therefore like to travel into the quiet land of faith, into the true realm of art."[4] The sentence is practically a quotation from Wackenroder: "Ah, thus I close my eyes to all worldly strife—and withdraw quietly into the land of music, as into the land of faith."[5] And it was Wackenroder to whom art religion, which received its name from Schleiermacher and its dogma from Tieck, was an original experience. He fulfilled the criterion he demanded of those "elected" to the "ordination" of art: that they "kneel down before art with upright hearts, and bring with them the homage of an eternal and unbounded love."[6] The origin of Wackenroder's art religion would seem to lie at least partially in the layer of pietism and *Empfindsamkeit* that was of central importance to the prehistory of romanticism as a whole. It is not difficult to recognize the language of the pietistic "Jesusminne"[7] in the second verse of the hymn in which Wackenroder's Joseph Berglinger worships Cecilia, patroness of music:

Thy wonderful tones
In which, enchanted, I indulge,
Have moved my spirit.
Dissolve my senses' fear;
Let me melt in song
That so delights my heart.[8]

The religious legacy, however—the almost manic alternation between trusting faith and despairing faith characteristic of Pietism—explains the vacillation between enthusiasm and depression that seems to endanger Wackenroder and Tieck's art religion.

In the sixth section of the *Fantasies on Art*, the "Letter of Joseph Berglinger" (which is the subject of philological controversy), exaltation to esthetic-religious devotion veers off suddenly into fear that the whole art religion is nothing more than a superstition: "From the firmest foundation of my soul, the cry welled up: It is a godly striving of man to create that which is not swallowed by any mean purpose and utility; that which is eternally resplendent in its own glory, independent of the world; that which is not driven by any cog of the great works, nor drives any other. No flame of the human breast rises higher, or truer to heaven, than art."[9] "Art is a deceitful, false superstition; we think we see the ultimate, innermost humanity in it, and yet it merely presents us with a beautiful human accomplishment, in which all the selfish, self-sufficient thoughts and perceptions that remain fruitless and inefficient in the active world are deposited."[10] (Tieck's comment that "among Berglinger's essays, the last four are mine"[11] was originally thought to reclaim the "Letter of Joseph Berglinger," the fourth piece from the end, for Tieck; but Richard Alewyn[12] argued that the allegorical poem "The Dream" that closes the *Fantasies on Art* must be counted as well, thus ascribing the "Letter" to Wackenroder.)

Whereas in the *Fantasies on Art* it is simply music itself, but especially the symphony, that Wackenroder and Tieck approach with religious devotion, E. T. A. Hoffman's enthusiasm appears curiously split: both Palestrina's vocal polyphony and Beethoven's symphonies are considered to be the highest musical expression of the "modern, Christian, romantic" age. Religious art and art religion seem to come into historical-philosophical competition with one another.

In the essay "Old and New Church Music," which Hoffman published in the Leipzig *Allgemeine Musikalische Zeitung* in 1814, five years after his review of Beethoven's Fifth Symphony, "holy musical art," whose historical period reached from Palestrina to Handel, appeared as something irretrievably in the past. Honoring Palestrina did not include an invitation to copy his style, as Eduard Grell and Michael Haller attempted in the nineteenth century,[13] but is instead connected to the insight that a restoration "from the inside out" would be impossible: "holy musical art" is a monument of memory, and it would be a vain undertaking to restore it in a present time that is no longer substantially Christian. "It would probably be quite impossible today for a composer to write as Palestrina, Leo, and later Handel, among others, did—as exquisitely as Christendom still shone in its full glory then, that age seems to have disappeared forever from the earth, and with it that consecration of its artists. No musician of today composes a Miserere the way Allegri or Leo did, just as no painter paints a Madonna like Raphael's, Dürer's, or Holbein's." But Hoffmann realizes the profound difference between painting and music, in that—to put it trenchantly—spiritual decay in painting introduced technical decay, whereas in music, the shriveling of Christian substance did not alter the fact that "obviously, the new musicians far exceed the old ones in technical skill." "Therefore the two arts, painting and music, present different aspects regarding their change and progress over time. Who may doubt that the great painters of that bygone age in Italy attained the highest level of art? The highest power and spirit lay in their works, and even in technical skill they exceeded the new masters, who strive in vain to attain it in any sense . . . but music is different."[14] However, the dialectic, that music gained in "art" or "skill" what it lost in "spirit" and "substantial interest," which reappears in Hegel's *Esthetics*, is not Hoffmann's last word on the music of modern times. Instead, he sees the differentiation of compositional technique as a path that abandons the "progress" of the "ruling spirit." (Hoffmann surpassed Hegel, who lacked immediate experience, in the insight that spirit in art is attached to technical detail; he refused to consider technical progress without spiritual development.) But the art in which the age around 1800 reached self-awareness is primarily instrumental music, the symphony. It replaces vocal music as the language in which one may immediately—without a longing backward glance—speak of the "wonders of the distant realm." "But music is different. The foolishness of human beings could not restrain the ruling spirit that progressed in darkness; and only he who could penetrate deeper, looking away from the sense-confounding image in which humanity, divorced from everything holy and true, moved, was able to see the rays that announced the presence of the spirit and broke through the darkness. Recognition of that wonderful striving, that working of the life-giving spirit of nature, even our existence in it, our home above the earth, that reveals itself in science, was suggested by the presaging tones of music, which spoke in ever more manifold and complete ways of the wonders of the distant realm. For it is certain that instrumental music has recently elevated itself to a level that the old masters never imagined, just as modern musicians obviously far exceed the old ones in technical skill."

One might be of the opinion that the "nature spirit" that reveals itself in the symphony must be distinguished sharply from the spirit of Christianity that was expressed by vocal polyphony. Yet "nature spirit" is also a religious category, and not just one of fairy tales. And as minimal as the theological weight of the "intimation of infinity" that Hoffmann extracted from his hearing of intrumental music might be, so profound was the meaning of his intuition for the history of ideas. Hoffmann's suggestion that a composer should not denigrate the modern richness of the instrumental side of modern church music was based on the idea that it was the "onward driving world spirit" that revealed itself in the instrumental music of "the newest age, which is working its way toward inner spiritualization." "Now, it is certain that music will hardly well up within a composer of today except in the adornments given it by the abundance of riches now available to him. The splendor of the manifold instruments, some of which sound so wonderful in high vaulting, shines forth everywhere: and why should one close one's eyes to it, as it is the onward driving world spirit itself that has cast this splendor into the mysterious art of the newest age, an age working its way toward inner spiritualization?"[15] Palestrina's "holy musical art" is not the only form of musical expression for religious consciousness. As the "world spirit" is an "onward driving" one, the accent within the concept of the "modern, Christian, romantic age" moves from the Christian to the romantic aspect. "The glory of Christianity," and with it "that holy blessing of artists," may have forever "disappeared from the earth," but Beethoven is the first "purely romantic (and precisely for that reason purely musical) composer."[16]

Thus it would seem that Hoffmann did not consider the loss of Christian substance to be the same as the decay of religious consciousness in general. Palestrina's "holy musical art" and Beethoven's instrumental music (which speaks of the "wonders of the distant realm") appear instead as musical forms of expression of different stages of development of a modern spirit, which Hoffmann, similarly to Hegel, perceived primarily in religious-philosophical categories. The "glory of Christianity" has been dissolved from vague "intimations of the infinite." But one would misunderstand Hoffmann by demoting the romantic expression of the religious to a deficient mode of Christianity or even denying its validity as a form of religious consciousness. Put bluntly, Beethoven's symphonies are "religious" music too, for they represent the stage of development at which a sharply defined Christianness is transformed into mere intimations of the "wonders of the distant realm" by the "onward driving world spirit," intimations that are nevertheless not a bare remnant of religion, but instead represent the religion of an "age working its way toward inner spiritualization." (Hoffmann was convinced that a "new church music" could come into being if composers would make the spirit of instrumental music, which is a religious spirit, their own, in order to compose works for a church in which Christian form has become a symbol for a religion whose substance lies beyond form in the unnameable.) "Ever further and further onward the ruling world spirit drives; the vanished forms, such as moved in physical pleasures, never return; but eternal, everlasting is that which is true, and a wonderful community of the soul wraps its mysterious band about past, present, and future."[17]

The hermeneutic model to which Hoffmann oriented himself in his music criticism—the concatenation of dichotomies such as "ancient-modern," "heathen-Christian," "classical-romantic," and "plastic-musical"—had its music-historical roots, as we have shown, in the debate over the *prima* and *seconda prattica*, and as far as the history of ideas is concerned, in the "Querelle des anciens et des modernes." In the early nineteenth century, both Hoffmann and Hegel interpreted the system of categories primarily in the sense of history of religion or philosophy of religion. The two entirely opposite art forms, ancient sculpture as the ideal of the "plastic," and the modern symphony as ideal of the "musical," appeared as manifestations of contrasting forms of religious consciousness. The Greek statue of a god is not a mere symbol of the god, but vouches for his immediate presence; religion manifests itself as art, and art as religion. (The term "art religion" in Hegel's *Phenomenology of the Spirit* of 1805 points to the "classical-ancient" merging of esthetic image and religious meaning, to the presence of one in the other; strictly speaking, Hegel's term, in contrast to Schleiermacher's, does not permit itself to be transferred to the Christian age, or to a secularized age still shaped by Christianity.)

In Christianity, the "idea" that determines the path of the development of art, and whose substance is the age's conception of God, withdraws from the externality of spatial, plastic manifestation into the "inwardness" of the prevailing self-awareness of the time, into "feeling." But in Hegel's system and philosophy of history, the art of "inwardness"—i.e., of the "modern, Christian, romantic age"—is music.

It seems reasonable to find the religious process of withdrawal into the inward reflected in the musical development of the disassociation from texts and firmly defined affections; that is, to refer, like E. T. A. Hoffmann, to "absolute" instrumental music as "mysterious art of the newest age, which is working its way toward inner spiritualization."[18] Yet Hegel's dialectic of "sounding inwardness," in whose context he interpreted modern instrumental music, is trickier than that. Hegel held fast to the tradition that the spirit was "word," and therefore let the philosophical history of art end with poetry and the odyssey of the world spirit end in philosophy; thus the simple formula that "absolute" music elevated itself to "intimations of the infinite," to "the absolute," by the very act of dissolving and liberating itself from the word, must have seemed to him deeply alien and suspicious of being mere enthusiasm. On the other hand, there was a tendency that expressed itself in the romantic metaphysics of instrumental music, and that was also contained in Hegel's esthetic system and train of thought as a partial force and would not let itself be suppressed.

"Mind is the infinite subjectivity of the idea, which as absolute inwardness is not capable of freely expanding in its entire independence so long as it remains within the mould of the bodily shape, fused therein as in the existence wholly congenial to it. To escape from such a condition the romantic type of art once more cancels that inseparable unity of the classical stage and its mode of expression. This content, if we may recall familiar ideas, is coincident with what Christianity affirms to be true as spirit, in contrast to the Greek faith in gods which forms the essential and most fitting content of classical art."[19] As "infinite subjectivity" or "absolute inwardness," the "mind" pushes on beyond the "objectivity" and "finiteness" of the ancient statue of a god—the art of a "plastic" age—that are perceived as a limitation. But in Hegel's philosophy, the motion of self-detachment, in which "inwardness" comes to itself, gets into a precarious and conflicting relationship with the firmness and substance that art has gained through Christianity. Hegel concedes that music, instead of grasping the "content" in a specific "meaning" as vocal music, has the possibility as instrumental music of merely expressing an indeterminate "atmosphere" called for or caused by the "content." "The inwardness, however, may be of twofold type. That is to say, to accept an object in its ideal presentation may, in the first place, mean that we do not conceive it in its actual appearance in the phenomenal world, but relative to its ideal significance. We may however mean by this, secondly, that a content is expressed as we find it realized in the experience of personal emotion."[20] If, however, music withdraws entirely from the representation of a "content" and into itself—and the tendency to do so is an innate characteristic of music, as it were—it becomes empty and abstract. "In recent times especially, the art of music, by its wresting itself from all content that is independently lucid, has withdrawn into the depths of its own medium. But on this very count and to this extent it has lost its compelling power over the soul, inasmuch as the enjoyment, which is thus offered, is only applicable to one aspect of art, in other words, is only an interest in the purely musical characteristics of the composition and its artistic dexterity, an aspect which wholly concerns the musical expert, and is less connected with the universal human interest in art."[21] "In such a case, however, music is empty, without significance, and is, for the reason that one fundamental aspect of art, namely spiritual content and expression, is absent, not really genuine art at all."[22] But for Hegel, hardly different from Hoffmann and, later on, Hanslick, it is precisely that music that tends toward abstraction, i.e., "absolute, pure music," that is the "real" music. "For musical expression therefore it is only the inner life of soul that is wholly devoid of an object that is appropriate, in other words, the abstract personal experience simply. This is our entirely empty ego, the self without further content."[23] What music loses as "art" that "pertains to the general human interest in art" it gains as music, as expression of the "self without further content." Insofar as music comes to itself, it distances itself from the "content" in which Hegel sees the foundation of its "cultural function." "The musician, on the contrary, it is true, does not abstract from all and every content, but finds the same in a text, which he sets to music, or with absolute freedom gives musical utterance to some definite mood in the form of a theme, which he proceeds to elaborate. The actual region, however, of his compositions remains the more formal ideality, in other words pure tones, and his absorption of content becomes rather a retreat into the free life of his own soul, a voyage of discovery into it, and in many departments of music even a confirmation that he as artist is free of the content."[24] The musical law of motion that the sentence retraces — the dialectic between "absorption" and "retreat" — seems to drive inexorably toward the abstraction that fulfills itself in "pure, absolute music."

The retreat of music into "inwardness" is thus a detachment and liberation in which it finds the way to itself, and simultaneously an emptying and formalization, a loss of substance. And that just the progressive abstraction "from all content that is independently lucid" — an abstraction that is practically mapped out as absolute music's historical trajectory — is to be comprehended as the sounding expression of an essentially religious experience, would be an interpretation that fed on the legacy of mysticism that Hegel, the philosopher of the "concrete," found deeply alien. Yet it is undeniable that the "retreat into the free life of his own soul," though it may ultimately lead into the vacuum, is the tendency within which the idea of absolute music converged with the spirit of Christianity as Hegel understood it. That the symphony was an emblem of the art religion of the Christian age was a concept that—despite Hegel's restriction of the concept of art religion to classical sculpture, and despite his Protestant mistrust of the notion of a language above language—lay concealed within the Hegelian esthetic without erupting to the surface.

In Hegel's esthetic, whose substance is a philosophy of history, the art forms from architecture to music and poetry array themselves about an elevated center, a *point de la perfection*. Classical art, whose paradigm is formed by the ancient sculpture of a god, differs from "symbolic" art, in which the unity of idea and appearance is not yet attained, and also from "romantic" art, in which that unity falls apart again because the spirit pushes on beyond the esthetic phenomenon instead of being realized in it.

As a countermove to Hegel, and simultaneously dependent on him, Christian Hermann Weisse, whose *System of Esthetics* appeared in 1830, i.e., between the "publication" of Hegel's esthetics as a cycle of lectures and their appearance in print, constructed a triadic scheme that has at its root the idea of progress toward the present, instead of the concept of an outstanding center belonging to the past. In Hegel's view, "romantic" art was above "classical" as a developmental stage of the mind, but was inferior as an esthetic phenomenon; for Weisse, the spiritually more developed art was simultaneously the esthetically more perfected one. However, this means nothing less than that the odyssey of the world spirit finds its completion in art (and not, as for Hegel, religion and philosophy, which the mind, when it leaves art behind, ultimately seeks).

Weisse separated the concept, formulated by August Wilhelm Schlegel, E. T. A. Hoffmann, and Hegel, of the "modern, Christian, romantic age," into its component parts; and from the "classical ideal" and the "romantic ideal" he distinguished a third stage, the "modern ideal." The historical philosophy of art forms, however, is based in the philosophy of religion, as with E. T. A. Hoffmann and Hegel: classical art is influenced by myth, romantic art by Christianity, and modern art—a "service of worship of pure beauty"—by a religious consciousness in which religion is art, and art religion. And the art form in which the "modern ideal" most purely manifests itself is "absolute" instrumental music. "Therefore instrumental music is the pure and immediate existence of the absolute or modern ideal, free of all specific structure—historically, too, it belongs entirely to this ideal; and even though it is conceptually the first art form, because it is the most abstract, it is the newest in its historical genesis."[25] Instrumental music is "free" and "absolute" because it has dissolved itself from meanings that adhere to music due to its origin in "natural sound" or speech. "The meaning that sound also possesses outside of music in nature or in the world of the human mind—the latter being the human voice and language—either remains excluded in this art, or, if it is incorporated, this can only happen by transmitting the idea that reveals itself as pure essentiality, free of all finite appearances, in tones inasmuch as they are tones and merely sounds."[26] Weisse formulates philosophically what E. T. A. Hoffmann expressed poetically: that as soon as affections, which are of themselves foreign to "pure music," nevertheless permeate music through song, they are "clothed in the crimson shimmer of romanticism."[27]

The "tone" in which, according to Weisse, the idea is manifested, is the "artificial" instrumental tone in contrast to the "natural sound" of the voice; and it is the "artificiality," to use Hanslick's term, that makes the musical material "comptetent to the spirit." "Tones, which through rhythm and harmony are combined into melody and into the musical work of art, are not immediately natural sounds but are produced through mechanical art; not merely in order to subordinate them externally to the will of the striving spirit that rules them, but also to purify them of all special, finite meaning that, as an alien content, would disturb and cloud the absolutely spiritual content with which they are to be imbued."[28] But the "pure concept of art"[29] that instrumental music realizes is, according to Weisse, a manifestation of religious consciousness; insofar as Weisse's theory of instrumental music anticipates Hanslickian formalism, it does so in the spirit of Hegel's philosophy of the absolute. "The vitality of the spirit, which displays its characteristic quality—different from all particulars inferior to the realm of beauty—in instrumental music, expresses itself in this art as an incessant surging or hovering between the two opposite poles of mourning and joy, or of lament and rejoicing, feelings and conditions that appear here in their pure form as attributes of the absolute or, if one chooses to use the term at this juncture, the godly spirit, without immediate reference to that which otherwise awakens, propagates, and accompanies them in the finite human mind. The way in which one could conceive the alternation of these conditions even within a being that is perfect and possesses eternity in the present (which would surely always stimulate a philosophy of the kind that could never attain the concept of the living godhead from the emptiness of its abstraction)—: it is just this art that teaches us of these things in a way more immediate than any other art or science."[30] Whereas Schopenhauer, in 1819, spoke of feelings in abstracto that are expressed by music, Weisse even elevates the objectless feelings divorced from earthly conditions into "attributes of the absolute, godly spirit": in a way similar to Wackenroder's, the metaphysics of instrumental music is rooted in an esthetic of feelings that seems "sacralized." (Likewise reminiscent of Wackenroder is Weisse's astonishment that the "mechanics" of artifical instruments is sufficient to bring forth the "wonders of music.") But the "feelings and conditions" that express themselves in absolute music are far removed from mundane affections. "All the common views of music that lag behind the concept of a purely ideal art, views that music is primarily the expression of subjective feelings, passions, etc., can only be forcefully applied to this music; because, in this case, the appearance of immediate causality through subjective feelings, which could produce this attitude in the case of song, falls away."[31] "Absolute" music, in which the "absolute" manifests itself, is just as dissolved from affections (as whose "language" an earlier esthetic attempted to justify it) as it is from texts and functions. But the "absolute" that it expresses is, in the "modern age," a religious idea that reveals itself as art. What Hegel said of the ancient statue of a god—that the religious idea is not merely "symbolized" but is immediately present in it—was transferred by Weisse to modern instrumental music. In it, the world history of art perfects itself; in the historical end, the ontological source comes to the fore. Whereas Hegel perceived the abstraction from content as a "hollowing out" of music, Weisse sees in it the truth of art. Weisse, a marginal figure in the history of philosophy, is the true apostle of an art religion that revolved around the idea of a "pure" art.

7

Musical Logic and Speech Character

An attempt to explain the idea of esthetic autonomy in exclusively sociohistorical terms, as a sign of withdrawal from the ugliness and coldness of an industrial world only then beginning to emerge, would fall short as a music-historical hypothesis. This is because, however pressing the socio-psychological motives might be, the idea of autonomy would remain a conceptual figment, its roots in the air, were there not an adequate object for the idea; and, as vocal music is "bound,"[1] that object had to be an instrumental music of recognized prestige. The impulse needed an object to which it could attach itself.

This in no way means, however, that instrumental music of the late eighteenth century was originally conceived as absolute music in the sense of romantic metaphysics. Instead, the symphonies of Carl Stamitz and Haydn were created in the context of a concert life that did not primarily strive for esthetic autonomy and metaphysical uplift, but for a communal culture of sentiment: a culture of sentiment closely related to the literary and pedagogical efforts of the bourgeoisie to understand itself and its humanitarian and moral resources. Haydn, as Georg August Griesinger reported, wished to depict "moral characters" in his symphonies; and the esthetic of representation was simultaneously intended as an esthetic of effect: put crudely, music, including instrumental music, existed to make itself useful as educational material. (And

Hermann Kretschmar was still assuming the early bourgeois concept of education when, around 1900, he attempted to rehabilitate the eighteenth-century esthetic of character and affection under the title of "musical hermeneutics": his polemic against the idea of absolute music was pedagogically motivated.)

Therefore, the interpretation of instrumental music in the spirit of the esthetic idea of autonomy is a reinterpretation. The change of interpretation that took place in romantic music esthetics, though, had to consider real and relevant characteristics of the matter itself so as not to remain groundless and thus historically ineffective. And the forces in compositional technique that made an "autonomization" of instrumental music possible may be summarized in the concept of "musical logic"—a concept closely connected to the notion of the "speech character" of music. That music presents itself as sounding discourse, as development of musical thoughts, is the compositional justification of its esthetic claim that it exists to be heard for its own sake: a claim that was nothing less than self-evident in the late eighteenth century.

In his "Fourth Grove of Criticism" of 1769, Johann Gottfried Herder still spoke of "logic" in music with unconcealed disdain. The philosophical exegete of music, as Herder imagined him, first immerses himself sympathetically in individual notes, which he perceives and understands as sounds of sentiment [*Empfindung*]. "At first nothing but simple, effective moments of music—single sounding accents of passion—that is the first thing he feels and gathers." Then the "main field of his observations" is melody; he connects the tones "by the bond of their sequence in their pleasantness for the ear, in their effect on the soul: that becomes melody." However, Herder dismisses the musical "logic" that lies in the context of the chords as a merely secondary force, although the "bond of sequence" in melody is hardly conceivable without harmony. (Herder had sided with Rousseau and against

104

Rameau in the music-esthetic debate over the precedence of melody or harmony.) "Harmony as such, as the moderns use the word, is to his"—the esthetician's—"esthetic only that which logic is to a poet; what fool would study it as his main purpose?"[2]

Not through Herder (who, it seems, was the first to use the term) but through Johann Nikolaus Forkel, two decades later, did the concept of musical logic gained music-esthetic respect. "Language is the garment of thought, just as melody is the garment of harmony. In this respect, one may call harmony a logic of music, because it stands in approximately the same relationship to melody as logic in language stands to expression, namely, it corrects and determines melodic writing so that it seems to become a real truth to one's sensations . . . Just as one expressed thoughts long before logic or an art of correct thinking existed in name, there were indeed melodies before one knew what was later called harmony by that name."[3] The phenomenon with which Forkel supported his argument was the simple fact that the expressive character of a melodic interval, say the minor sixth D-B-flat, is partly dependent on the harmonic-tonal context, that is, on whether it is the fifth and third in G minor or the third and tonic in B flat major. However, Forkel assumed the older theory of speech that saw language merely as a medium for formulating and "clothing" the contents of thoughts and feelings that already existed for themselves. According to Forkel, melodies are sounding manifestations—musical formulations—of perceptions that make up the content and sense of music. Forkel, like Herder, began with the esthetic quality of the single tone as sound of sentiment [*Empfindung*], but, in contrast to Herder, he recognized the conditions of a more determined, richer, more differentiated musical expression of feelings in a harmonically regulated tonal system. Where Herder contrasted, he mediated. And he named the harmonic regulation of tonal relations "musical logic," because through it the signs for perceptions are brought into "true"—i.e., corresponding to the nature of the thing—relation to one another, similar to the way in which the signs for things and concepts are treated in language. Harmony is a "prerequisite" for the "truth and determinacy" of musical expression.[4]

What Ludwig Tieck, who had heard Forkel's lectures in Göttingen, says about the effect of modern instrumental music in the 1799 *Fantasies on Art* is first of all a reflection of Forkel's thesis that there exists in music a hidden logic that permeates and regulates the sounding expression of feeling. "Here it occurs that one thinks thoughts without any tiresome detour through words; here feeling, fantasy, and the power of thought are one."[5] In Tieck's rhapsody "Tones," however, the relationship between the language of thoughts and that of tones appears in a different light: in both languages, the unspeakable, which is not immediately comprehensible through either words or tones, is what is actually and ultimately meant; and perhaps tones come closest to the incomprehensible, despite a remnant of insufficiency. "Man is generally so proud to have been endowed with the ability to put a system in words and extend it, that he can set down in common speech those thoughts that seem finest and most daring to him. But . . . the greater man perceives only too well that his innermost thoughts are but a tool, that his reason and its conclusions are still dependent on the essence that is himself and that he will never completely comprehend during this life. Is it therefore not irrelevant whether he thinks in instrumental sounds or in so-called thoughts? In either one he can but play and tinker about; and music, as the darker and finer language of the two, will often surely satisfy him more than the other."[6] The unspeakable on which Tieck meditates is neither feeling nor thought, but rather something substantial beyond the differences that are imposed upon us by our system of categories. For Tieck, the relationship of thought to feeling, in which Forkel had located the concept of musical logic (the "truth and determinacy" of musical expression of feeling), dissolves into metaphysics.

Accordingly, if romantic esthetics, which recognized "pure, absolute music" in instrumental music, was destructive on the onehand, it produced on the other a changed concept of musical logic. "All pure music," wrote Friedrich Schlegel sometime between 1797 and 1801, "must be philosophical and instrumental (music for thought)."[7] And in one of the fragments of his *Athenäum* he writes, in a passage that could be a commentary on the aforegoing laconic note: "Some find it strange and foolish when musicians speak of the thoughts in their compositions . . . But whoever has a sense of the affinities among all the arts and sciences will at least not view the matter from the uninspired viewpoint of naturalness, according to which music is only supposed to be the language of feelings, and will not find a certain tendency of all pure instrumental music toward philosophy to be impossible of itself. Must not pure instrumental music itself create a text of its own? And does not its theme get developed, confirmed, varied, and contrasted like the object of meditation in a philosophical sequence of ideas?"[8] Having moved instrumental music from the sphere of the communal culture of sentiments to the exaltedness of an abstraction whose sense is derived from solitary esthetic contemplation, Schlegel could no longer seek musical "logic," which autonomous music needed for its esthetic justification, in Forkel's concept of "harmony" as the constitutive element of the musical expression of sentiment: the theory of instrumental music emphasized melodic, rather than harmonic, logic in its legitimizing esthetic.

In musical reality, harmonic and thematic structure were inseparable: emancipated instrumental music was constituted as sounding discourse through a logic that was determined simultaneously by theme and harmony working as one. The modern concept of form, which developed around 1700 in the operatic and cantata aria, and above all in the instrumental concerto, is based both on the principle of harmonic tonality, which, as the general aspect of music, sketches an outline; and on the thematic principle, the specific aspect of music, from which development proceeds. Tonal disposition and thematic process are the components of a musical form capable of existing esthetically on its own, without benefit of text or function, as a broad, differentiated, and nevertheless unbroken, internally coherent process. The closure of the form is the correlate of the autonomy of the work.

Thus a movement of, say, a concerto by Antonio Vivaldi is based on a ritornello that no longer functions as a frame, but as a theme (and which Johann Mattheson in 1739 characterized as analogous to the propositio of a legal argument).[9] The transposition of the ritornello into various keys, and modulatory developments in the episodes between the stable key areas of the ritornello, produce a harmonically based formal scaffolding: a scaffolding that lets the comparison between music and architecture, which has become a commonplace, seem plausible. On the other hand, parts of the theme may be isolated, varied, or regrouped, so that there emerge the beginnings of the process that later on, as thematic-motivic work in Haydn and Beethoven, became the epitome of discursive musical logic. And the difference between thematic exposition or recapitulation and motivic work is closely related to the tonal foundation of the form, because thematic and tonal closures are related to one another in the same way as are motivic and modulatory development. (At the same time one should not ignore that, along with the "logic" in Vivaldi, other, older justifications of instrumental music, such as the showcasing of virtuosity and the tone-painting representation of programmatic subjects, were of no little importance.)

Schlegel's aphorism was but a fleeting spark of anticipation. Not until half a century later, in Eduard Hanslick's treatise *On the Beautiful in Music*, were the concepts of form and theme moved firmly into the center of music esthetics (and not merely of the study of form); and his esthetic was nothing more or less than an esthetic of absolute music. (According to Hanslick, texts are interchangeable, programs irrelevant.) Hanslick depends on the romantic metaphysics of instrumental music insofar as he declared instrumental music to be the "true" music and sharpened Tieck's distancing of instrumental music from the affective expression of vocal music into a polemic against the "decayed esthetic of sentiment;" however, it seems as though in 1854, at a time of philosophical sobering after the downfall of Hegelianism, the metaphysical substance of the esthetics of the beginning of the century was spent. "Devotion" before the "wonders of music" yielded to a dry empiricism that insisted on a scientific attitude. According to Hanslick, the nature of music is to be sought in its "specifically musical" aspects: not in the "poetic" character it has in common with other arts, but in the sounding form by which it distinguishes itself from them.

Nonetheless, one should take care not to rush into an interpretation of Hanslick. What may seem like a detour is in fact the most direct approach. Hanslick, the easily comprehensible writer, must be seen relative to Hegel, the difficult-to-understand philosopher, if one wishes to comprehend seriously what Hanslick actually meant, and wherein the problem he sought to solve consisted. "To the question: What is to be expressed with this musical material? the answer is: Musical ideas. A fully realized musical idea, however, is already something beautiful by itself, is its own purpose, and is in no way merely means or material for the representation of feelings and thoughts . . . Tonally moving forms are the sole content and object of music."[10] Hanslick's famed dictum, quoted to excess, that the form of music determines its content, is not a thesis utterly comprehensible of itself, but a paradox that can only be made comprehensible by reconstructing the polemical situation out of which it was formulated. It would be a gross simplification to reduce the dialectic point to the triviality that music is form and nothing else. (However, the success of the thesis, as measured in the frequency of its quotation, seems to be based on the fact that one can conceive it in the banal sense and simultaneously flaunt its paradoxical formulation.) In the historical context of ca. 1850, Hanslick's doctrine implies an exposure to Hegelianism, the reigning philosophy of the 1830s and 1840s. (To be precise, the exposure was to the Hegelianism that had entered the common parlance of intellectuals rather than to Hegel's actual texts.) Hegel had defined the beautiful as the "physical manifestation of the idea" [*sinnliches Scheinen der Idee*]. ("Scheinen" here means both "to appear" and, in the Neoplatonic tradition, "to shine forth.") And Hanslick adopted the difference between idea and appearance in order to be able to define the beautiful in music, the subject of his treatise; unlike Hegel, however, he did not determine the sounding phenomenon to be appearance and "thoughts and feelings" to be idea or (as Hegel also said) content, but rather sought the idea or content in the specifically musical aspect. The "idea," however, which appears as "musical idea" in the musical material, Hanslick called "form." In his esthetic, form is therefore not the manifested form, but the form of the nature of the thing: "inner form," as the ancient term, which Shaftesbury introduced into modern esthetics, is called. And the dictum regarding "tonally moving forms" that are supposed to serve as "content" therefore means that sounding form— the acoustical substrate—represents the phenomenal element, whereas the form is the ideal, content-laden element. Form, as Hanslick understands it, is not the exterior but the interior, and in that sense "content" (in the Hegelian sense, used only for the sake of polemical contrast). "The forms that form themselves out of tones are . . . spirit manifesting itself from the inside out."[11] "Composing is a working of the spirit in material capable of [sustaining] the spirit" *(geistesfähigem Material).*[12] This does not mean that Hanslick considers musical form, as traditionally conceived, to be spirit, but that, inversely, he determines the spirit in music to be form. The decisive condition of Hanslick's conception of form is the Hegelian concept of content—reversed into its opposite—and not the tradition of music theory. On the other hand, Hanslick's concept of musical form implies the two components that are connected to one another in the romantic idea of absolute music: form is specifically musical, dissolved from extra-musical determinations and in that respect "absolute"; and for just this reason, however, it is not only a manifested form, but spirit, essential form, form created from the inside out.

Hanslick used the theme as example. "In every musical composition, the independent, esthetically indivisible, musical unit of thought is the theme. The primitive determinations which one ascribes to music as such must always be demonstrable in the theme, the musical microcosm . . . What, then, shall one designate as content? The tones themselves? Certainly, for they alone are already formed. And what is form? Again, the tones themselves—but they are already fulfilled form."[13] The theme is paradigmatic of what Hanslick calls "form," because it is a whole made of parts and simultaneously part of a whole, thus indicating that form must be determined as "energeia," as "spirit manifesting itself from the inside out": as a process in which material enters into a coherence of meaning that in turn is material for a more comprehensive coherence of meaning. From the concept of theme the idea of thematic process as "meditation" or "sequence of ideas" arises, as Friedrich Schlegel put it—the idea that represented the epitome of musical form in the nineteenth century.

Hanslick's altered conception of musical form, which interpreted it as essential rather than manifested form, is closely connected to a concept of the speech character of music that diverges substantially from Forkel's concept of "tonal language." "In music there is sense and consequence, but of a musical kind; it is a language that we speak and understand, but are incapable of translating. There is a profound meaning in the fact that one also speaks of 'ideas' in musical works, and, just as in speech, a practiced judge can easily distinguish true ideas from mere clichés."[14] Like Forkel, Hanslick considers musical logic—"sense and consequence"—to be analogous to speech. But he is not thinking of the harmonic regulation and differentiation of musical "sounds of sensibility"— the "decayed esthetic of sentiment" is the object of his loathing; instead, he is thinking of an "intramusical" logic.

However, Hanslick seems to have gotten the idea of a "spirit" of language, manifesting itself in the language's "form," from Wilhelm von Humboldt. (He quotes not Humboldt but Jacob Grimm,[15] who shared the relevant premises of linguistic theory with Humboldt.) According to Humboldt, language—to put it in Hanslick's words, which are very nearly Humboldt's own—is "a working of the spirit in material capable of the spirit." And Humboldt called the inner structure that prefigures the paths of a language conceived as activity of the spirit the "form of language." "Within this working of the spirit—the exaltation of articulated sound to the expression of thought, that which is constant and uniform, when expressed as completely as possible in its context and represented systematically, makes up the form of language."[16] Speech is not manifested as mere "clothing" of thoughts and feelings, as in the older theory of language predicated by Forkel, but as spriritual activity that forms and does not simply formulate. "[Language] itself is not a kind of work *(ergon)* but an activity *(energeia)*. Its true definition can therefore only be a genetic one. Namely, it is the ever-repeating labor of the spirit to make the articulated sound competent to express thought."[17] Although Humboldt refers to the "inner form" of a language as a whole, whereas Hanslick is discussing individual musical works, this difference changes nothing in the correspondence of the relevant categories (which, moreover, are also valid in Humboldt for the "working of the spirit" in details of language): a correspondence that allowed Hanslick to designate music as a language without having to revert to the doctrine that it was a "language of sentiment." If speech is not merely "clothing," but "inner form," a "working of the spirit" in "articulated sound," then music, in which "the forms that form themselves out of tones are .. . . spirit manifesting itself from the inside out," can be designated as a language in an almost unmetaphorical sense. Accordingly, Humboldt's philosophy of language was one of the fundamental precepts of the Hanslickian thesis (that music as form was "spirit," i.e., "content" in the Hegelian sense) that made it superfluous to search for content outside of form, in sentiments or affections, in order to designate music as "physical manifestation of the idea," as musically beautiful. Only before the background of the romantic metaphysics of absolute music, of Humboldt's linguistic theory, and of the Hegelian dialectic of nature and appearance, does Hanslick's theory of form, seemingly a straightforwardly empirical category, take on shape and color.

Søren Kierkegaard, whose esthetic is actually an anti-esthetic, did not actually deny the speech character of music—the esthetic justification of autonomous instrumental music—but perceived it as crumbling. In an argument of extreme dialectic complexity, Kierkegaard takes up motives from the theory of absolute music in order, after a fleeting gesture of seeming agreement, to let them drop and shatter unexpectedly. At the same time, the romantic idea that music is the characteristic art of the Christian age falls into a twilight in which the "holy art" distorts itself into a "demonic" one.

"But a medium which is spiritually determined is essentially language; since therefore music is spiritually determined, it has justly been called a language."[18] The

difference, constitutive for a language, between the represented and the present, between the meaning and its
medium, seems to recur in music. "But it is different in the
case of language. The sensuous is reduced to a mere
instrument, and is thus annulled . . . So it is also with
music: that which really should be heard constantly
emancipates itself from the sensuous."[19] Nonetheless,
music is a lower language because of the indeterminacy of
that which it says or stammers. It "always expresses the
immediate in its immediacy; it is for this reason, too, that
music shows itself first and last in relation to language"[20]
first, because a language that descends to its origins arrives
at interjections, which "in turn are musical"; last, insofar
as a lyric language finally attains a stage at which "at last
the musical has been developed so strongly that language
ceases and everything becomes music."[21] But the "immediate," the medium of music, is suspect to Kierkegaard—
no differently than it was to Hegel; and the "indeterminacy" in which music without text loses itself is in no
way—as "intimation of infinity"—a distinction, but a
defect. "The immediate is really the indeterminate, and
therefore language cannot apprehend it; but the fact that it
is indeterminate is not its perfection, but an
imperfection."[22] Absolute music is indeed a language, but
one that stands beneath, not above, the language of words.
"This is the reason why I never had any sympathy, and in
this perhaps even the experts will agree with me, for the
more sublime music which believes it can dispense with
words. As a rule it thinks itself higher than words, although
it is really inferior."[23]

Kierkegaard calls the "immediate" that music expresses
"sensuous immediacy." (This does not mean the "sensuous" as matter for perception, from which the "truly"
musical "constantly emancipates itself," but the "erotic
sensual genius," whose paradigm was, to Kierkegaard,
Mozart's *Don Giovanni*.)[24] Under the rule of Christianity,

however, the sensuous appears as that which lies outside the spirit; and, being excluded, it is "demonic."[25] But that which is negated by the spirit—Kierkegaard is employing Hegel's "determined negation"—is "spiritually determined." And insofar as spiritual determinacy guarantees the speech character of music, music is a language only as a negation of language. (As interjection it is "not yet" music; as dissolution of lyricism into sonic magic, it is "no longer" music.)

The thesis that Kierkegaard destroyed philosophically (out of secretly theological motives)—that music, specifically and especially instrumental music, is a language above language—was restored philosophically (and with manifest theology, albeit one that was rather more conjured up than "believed") a century later by Theodor W. Adorno. "As opposed to language that means something, music is language of a completely different type. In that type lies its theological aspect. What it says is an appearance simultaneously determined and hidden. Its idea is the form of the name of God. It is . . . the human attempt, though futile as always, to speak the name itself, not to impart meanings."[26] Music "refers to the true language as to one in which the content itself becomes manifest, but at the price of unequivocalness, which passed to the 'meaningful' languages."[27] The language of Jewish theology, which Adorno borrowed from the poetic and linguistic theory of Walter Benjamin, could, however, be exchanged for a dialectic-metaphysical one without loss of meaning, one in which a faint echo of romantic music esthetics is audible, though the once-enthusiastic "intimation of infinity" is dampened by the disappointment over the fact that one will not get beyond mere intimations. "Meaningful language would like to speak the absolute in a mediated way, but it slips away in every single intention, leaves each one be-hind as finite. Music achieves it immediately, but at the same moment it becomes dark, just as over-intense light blinds the eye, leaving it unable to see what is completely visible."[28]

In order to initiate a philosophical understanding in less metaphorical terms of an absolute music that he perceived as language above language, Adorno invoked the "transcendency of musical specificity" on the one hand, and "intermittent intentions" on the other. "Every musical phenomenon points beyond itself, due to what it reminds one of, what it contrasts with, whereby it awakens expectations. The epitome of such transcendency of musical specificity is 'content': that which happens in music."[29] This formulation, which is left hanging in the balance, does not completely obscure the equivocal use of the word "transcendency": it refers simulatneously to an internal, formal characteristic, and to an external one. That musical details "point beyond themselves"—that tones and motives only constitute themselves as music through the context in which they stand, rather than remaining mere coustic phenomena—says nothing conclusive about a "sense" of music that "points beyond" its structure. The concept of "intermittent intention"[30] means that semantic elements of a music that attempts to avoid both the wheel-spinning of the merely structural and dependence on extramusical programs may neither be absent nor merge into a ubiquitous "layer" (to use Roman Ingarden's term). Instead, it sporadically "flares up." But Adorno endows fleeting intuition, such as music supplies at some moments, with a trust he withholds from an "instrumentalized language corrupted by decayed social practice."

8

On the Three Cultures of Music

In a letter to his mother of July 15, 1850, Hans von Bülow reported the musical tendencies of the Berlin court: "Meyerbeer immediately counseled me to play an opera fantasy, because the familiar Italian melodies had the approval of the queen and the court. Only before the king might I play what I pleased, even Bach and Beethoven."[1] The king's taste, however, would seem to reflect that which had gained acceptance among the bourgeoisie some decades before. Robert Schumann noted in "Master Raro's, Florrestan's, and Eusebius's Booklet of Thoughts and Poems" (1833): "I see nothing extraordinary in the fact that one is beginning to value the things of Bach and Beethoven in Berlin."[2]

The formula "Bach and Beethoven," whose far-reaching consequences for the history of ideas Schumann could hardly have predicted, differs from such groupings as "Bach and Handel" or "Haydn, Mozart, and Beethoven" in that it is based on historical-philosophical considerations rather than historical-stylistic ones. To begin with, it reflects the canonical works of the most demanding piano literature (while ignoring Bach's primary role as a composer of vocal music): the *Well-Tempered Clavier* and the Beethoven sonatas from Op. 2 through Op. 111, i.e., the "Forty-eight" and the "Thirty-two," as they were later known in England.[3] Above and beyond that, however, Bach and Beethoven, exalted above all other composers, quite simply represented the tradition of great music, the tradition in which Schumann, writing his manifesto "For the Opening of the Year 1835" of the *Neue Zeitschrift für Musik*, sought support in order to "combat the inartistic recent past" and "prepare a new poetic era."[4] "A magazine for 'music yet to come' is still wanting," wrote Schumann before founding such a journal. "Only men like the late, blinded Cantor of the Thomasschule or the deaf Kapellmeister laid to rest in Vienna would be suitable as its editors."[5] Bach and Beethoven were praised as rulers of the "spirit world" that E. T. A. Hoffmann had declared instrumental music to be; and what they held in common was the "poetic" element that Ludwig Tieck had recognized as the nature of "pure, absolute music." "Of course, if I thought of the highest kind of music, such as Bach and Beethoven have given us in individual works; if I spoke of rare mental states to be revealed by the artist; if I demanded that each of his works take a step further into the spirit-world of art; if, in a word, I demanded poetic depth and novelty everywhere, in every part as in the whole: then I would have a long search, nor would any of the works I have mentioned, or most works currently appearing, satisfy me."[6] Only in scattered works does the "new poetic era" announce itself. But Schumann completes the three-part historical-philosophical schema, in which a decayed immediate past—the epoch of the *juste-milieu*—is contrasted with a golden age whose return is marked by the present, with the dialectic thought that the present, as a "new poetic era," might have the mission of mediating between divergent tendencies of the great past—between the deep intellect of Bach and the sublimity of Beethoven. "Where Bach delves ever deeper, so deep that even the miner's light threatens to go out in the depths, where Beethoven reaches up into the clouds with his Titanic fist, what the most recent era, which would reconcile heights and depths, has endeavored, of all this the artist is aware."[7] Tradition, overpowering though it may seem, does not have the last word.

Richard Wagner gave the combination of Bach and Beethoven a nationalistic accent. Whereas Beethoven's symphonic works had always—since the early enthusiasm for the Ninth Symphony—represented the epitome of music itself, Bach, representative of the "German spirit" in "wretched times," was placed beside Beethoven in the essay "What is German?" (published in 1878, though the main portions were written in 1865).[8] From the formula "Bach and Beethoven," originally a grouping of classicists of keyboard music, there evolved the "myth of German music" to which Arnold Schoenberg still adhered when, in 1923, he declared that the discovery of the dodecaphonic system had secured the supremacy of German music for the time being. (Schoenberg considered himself an heir to Bach and Beethoven.)

Schumann's utopian idea that in a "new poetic age" replacing the era of decay it must be possible for heterogeneous tendencies of the past, namely, Bach's contemplative depth and Beethoven's Promethean sublimity, to interpenetrate, recurred in various guises—that is, with varying notions of who was ordained to represent the "new poetic age"—in the later nineteenth and twentieth centuries. However varied the three-part schemata that people designed in their historical-philosophical exuberance (Bülow argued for Bach, Beethoven, and Brahms, Nietzsche for Bach, Beethoven, and Wagner, August Halm for Bach, Beethoven, and Bruckner), the idea of a German epoch in music was always latent in the background, and it was always in the name of the idea of "pure, absolute music" that one created an array of composers that was intended to justify nothing less than a philosophy of music history. (As mentioned, Nietzsche considered Wagner's music drama to be "absolute music" in the sense of Schopenhauer's metaphysics.)

In *The Birth of Tragedy out of the Spirit of Music* of 1871, Nietzsche wrote: "Out of the Dionysian root of the German spirit, a power has arisen which, having nothing in common with the original conditions of Socratic culture," — meaning the rationalistic culture opposite the Dionysian one — "can neither be explained nor excused by it, but which is rather felt by this culture as something terribly inexplicable and overwhelmingly hostile — German music as we must understand it, particularly in its vast solar orbit from Bach to Beethoven, from Beethoven to Wagner."[9] The national pathos, to which Nietzsche seldom tended otherwise, derived from Wagner, as did the formula "from Bach to Beethoven." And even the practical substance of the three-part scheme can be found in Wagner's theory, for the compositional and esthetic correlate of the thought that the tradition of great music extended from Bach via Beethoven to Wagner consists of none other than the principle of "endless melody." In the 1870s, after Liszt and, later, Josef Rubinstein had played him preludes and fugues of Bach, Wagner several times said that "endless melody was already formed in the *Well-Tempered Clavier*."[10] And in the essay "Music of the Future," in which the term "endless melody" was coined,[11] it is not his own music dramas but Beethoven's symphonies in which Wagner first finds the principle revealed. A movement such as the first movement of the *Eroica* is "none other than a single, perfectly cohering melody."[12]

It should not be disconcerting to find that Wagner discovered the prehistory of "endless melody" in instrumental music, for in a music drama the orchestra is the primary bearer of the "endless melody." And, without lapsing into speculative arbitrariness, one may even tighten the connection between the idea of absolute music and the principle of "endless melody" by recognizing as a trivial misunderstanding the notion that the "endlessness" of the melody consists in its avoidance or elision of cadences and caesuras, and attempting to reconstruct the original meaning of the term. According to Wagner, music is "melodic" when every note is eloquent and expressive; and in contrast to a "narrow melody," in which the melodic element is continually interrupted in order to make room for vacuous formulae, an "endless melody" is at all times "melodic" in the emphatic sense of the word, without being interrupted by cliches, fillers, and empty gestures. (The avoidance of cadences is not the nature of the principle, but one of its consequences: cadences are formulae, thus they are not "melodic.")

Accordingly, the principle of "endless melody" rests on the esthetic premise that music, as Eduard Hanslick put it, is a "language" in which "a practiced judge easily distinguishes true ideas from mere clichés."[13] But the music to which Hanslick attributed the character of speech was "pure, absolute music," which only gained esthetic legitimacy as an autonomous art form by being a "musical language."

In Wagner's philosophy of music history, it was Beethoven who developed the speech capacity of instrumental music to the point at which musical expression, instead of being limited to feelings in the abstract, attained individual determinacy; albeit a determinacy that finally demanded words in the Ninth Symphony, as it had become internally contradictory, being pointlessly determinate, an individualized expression without an object.[14] (Whereas Wagner ascribed an individually determined speech capacity exclusively to Beethoven in the 1851 "Opera and Drama," he later, in the 1870s, recognized Bach as well for his importance in the development of the character of speech in instrumental music, as one may conclude from Wagner's statements about Bach's "endless melodies.")

Wagner, having converted to Schopenhauer's metaphysics of music, which was a theory of absolute music, did not expressly reject the thesis that the speech capacity of instrumental music required "redemption" through words and scenic processes (in order to escape the dilemma of saying specific things but in incomprehensible form) but he did modify it radically. After all, that the orchestral melody in a music drama expresses the nature and inner quality of both action and words—that it therefore represents a language behind the language of the drama—bespeaks nothing less than that the "unredeemed" language of instrumental music is the "true" language of a music that is a tool of metaphysics. (The language of words never approaches that which music expresses, but is simply its reflection in the categories of the "world of appearances.") This does not, however, rule out that, according to Wagner, musical language—from which the Schopenhauerian "will" speaks—is dependent on the language of words as an empirical correlate, in order to become effective at all as an organon of metaphysics. In other words: texts and scenic processes may be mere bridges to metaphysical contemplation through the spirit of music, but they are bridges whose necessity should not be denied, even though one may insist on tearing them down after crossing them. On the other hand, the indispensability of an empirical correlate to metaphysical elevation through absolute music, which Wagner postulated in his open letter "On Franz Liszt's Symphonic Poems," changes nothing in his principal concession—motivated by his appropriation of Schopenhauer and his experiences in composing *Tristan*—that metaphysical music, which has the last word beyond words, is absolute music. The idea of an "endless" melody, always eloquent and meaningful, is therefore tendentially—applied to orchestral melody that is substance and not accompaniment within a music drama—an example of absolute-music esthetics: not of the phenomenon that Hanslick meant, but of the idea at which Schopenhauer aimed.

Whereas the music drama, as Nietzsche realized, was secretly absolute music, Ernst Bloch actually spoke of a "purification of Wagner" by Bruckner, who rehabilitated the symphony, declared dead by Wagner, in the musical language of Wagnerian orchestral melody. "Recently, Bruckner has found a devoted interpreter of his ability and his situation in August Halm. He has shown that Bruckner provides what Beethoven could not; in Beethoven, the element of song was lost in the great arch, in the energy-filled motive and the power to control masses. Because Bruckner has achieved this, the impure spur of poetic causes simultaneously becomes forever superfluous; in fact, what this master has done is to separate the gain in the Wagnerian style, the 'speaking' music, from the cost of tuition, so to speak, that the program or music drama represented, and thereby reconstitute music as actuality, as form and content at once, as a road to seas other than that of poetry."[15] Just as the symphony had appeared as "unredeemed" music drama in Wagner's historical mythology, Halm and Bloch, in a countermove no less violent, describe music drama as merely the "cost of tuition": as the not yet emancipated symphony. As Wagner reclaimed the musical powers of speech of the Beethovenian symphony for music drama, Bruckner assimilated the musical language of the music drama for the symphony. The formula "Bach, Beethoven, and Bruckner" came into being as specific negation of Nietzsche's "Bach, Beethoven, and Wagner."

August Halm, whom Bloch consulted, quoted, and paraphrased, spoke of "two cultures of music" in the title of his most famous book (1913); he saw them as represented by Bach's fugues and Beethoven's sonatas. But the driving idea of the book, by which the antithesis of Bach and Beethoven gained relevance instead of remaining a historical construct, was that of a "third culture," whose outlines Halm found drawn in Bruckner's symphonies: outlines in which the path was prefigured for later composers (among whom Halm counted himself) without their having, therefore, to consider themselves epigones in the pejorative sense of the word. "A third culture, the synthesis of the two we have attempted to depict in this book, is to be expected; it will be a complete culture of music for the first time, and no longer just one culture of many, and I believe it has been founded, perhaps already attained. I see it germinating and living in Anton Bruckner's symphonies."[16] Halm, who derived an analytic technique from Eduard Hanslick's esthetic, draws the concepts of form and theme, in which Hanslick recognized the constitutive categories of absolute music, into a dialectic in which they primarily form a historical antithesis. Halm contrasts a "culture of the theme" in Bach's fugues with a "culture of form" in Beethoven's sonatas. Put trenchantly, the form in a fugue is a function of the theme; in the sonata the theme is, inversely, a function of form. (And one may doubt whether the fugue is a form at all, or merely a technique.) "Basically, the fugue is dominated by a law: this is simply its theme, whose individual characteristics, its virtues, are to be shown to advantage in it . . . in contrast, sonata form shows more of a course of action; this is served by the principal themes and the way in which they are developed."[17] Put in the terminology of dramatic theory: whereas form in the fugue arises from the character of the thematic matter, in the sonata the thematic matter is subject to the "fate" that the form imposes upon it. The outline of the music-esthetic "Querelle" of the eighteenth century—the debate about the preeminence of melody or harmony—stands out as the background in the history of ideas in the antithesis developed by Halm. For the "culture of the theme" that Halm praises in Bach's fugues is nothing but the art of melody: the art, which he demonstrates in the theme of the Fugue in B-flat minor from the second book of the *Well-Tempered Clavier*, of letting a melodic construction appear as a closed system of tonal relations supported in itself, in which ever-richer differentiation leads to ever-denser integration.[18] Likewise, the "culture of form" that Beethoven founded is primarily an art of "harmonic economy": in Beethoven[19] the entry of a tonality represents an "event" from which compelling consequences arise, while Bach introduces new keys almost unnoticeably, "with a calm hand," without making the process of form, whose support is the harmony, noticeable. In other words, the theme is substantial in the fugue, but the form "is not yet alive": in the sonata, a "life of the form" develops, but the thematic matter often remains without substance.

In Halm's 1913 work, his praise of Bruckner, the representative of a "third culture of music," took the shape of a secretly polemical challenge to Beethoven worship, then still overwhelming and sacrosanct. "Bruckner is the first absolute musician of great style and complete mastery since Bach, the creator of dramatic music—which is the enemy and the conquerer of music drama. If the fugue wanted to be fertilized by the spirit of the new music, it had to create contrast in the manner of treating the theme while leaving its thematic unity intact."[20] "Dramatic music," as seen by Halm, is a dialectic, symphonic style determined by contrasts, in which contrasts enter such that "they become events."[21] And Bruckner's symphonic style is the "conqueror of music drama," and not only its "enemy" in that it incorporates the "dramatic" instead of letting it continue alongside it as a constituent of a "different culture of music."

The interpenetration of fugue and sonata form that Halm postulates and finds realized in Bruckner is not solely a technical-formal intermingling, as in the finale of the Fifth Symphony, but, above and beyond that, an appropriation by the sonata of the "thematic culture" developed in the fugue: an appropriation that characterizes the whole of Bruckner's works, not just single movements.

The conditions that made a "third culture of music" possible, however, were discovered by Halm in modern harmony as shaped by Wagner. "Bruckner, a harmonist in his heart and blood, finds in his highly developed harmony a new purpose, a new content for melody. Not a service to form, to something superordinate, but something with which it could create in itself, with which it gained support and tension, became capable of great dimension, broad arches, daring curves."[22] Halm's book on Bruckner is nothing less than an attempt to demonstrate analytically that Bruckner's harmony was able to give backing and substance to a striding melodic style that rises above Beethoven's melodically rudimentary style of sonata theme with a grand sweep reminiscent of Bach, without simultaneously narrowing tonality's power to create and bear a broad symphonic coherence and make obvious the "periods of the form." (A way of listening that perceives a similar "progression" in Bachian melody to Wagnerian and Brucknerian melody was later described in more detail and esthetically codified by Ernst Kurth. Kurth's main works, a book on Bach as a counterpoint treatise, one on Wagner as a harmony treatise, and one on Bruckner as a treatise on form, represent as a whole a theory and esthetic of absolute music— according to Wagner himself, harmony is the force that constitutes music "for itself"— that is negatively characterized by its exclusion of Beethoven.)

Anton Webern, who strove for an interpenetration of fugal polyphony and sonata form in his Symphony, Op. 21, expressed what Schoenberg's school as a whole claimed for itself when, in his lecture series *The Path to New Music*, he included both the tradition of Bach, which looks back to the Netherlanders of the fifteenth and sixteenth centuries, and the tradition of Beethoven as epitome of the classical, in the prehistory of dodecaphony. "So the style Schoenberg and his school are seeking is a new interpenetration of music's material in the horizontal and the vertical . . . It's not a matter of reconquering or reawakening the Netherlanders, but of refilling their forms by way of the classical masters, of linking these two things. Naturally it isn't purely polyphonic thinking; it's both at once."[23]

That it must be possible to think melodically-polyphonically in the spirit of Bach and the Netherlanders and simultaneously harmonically-formally in the sense of Beethoven's conception of the sonata, that, in other words, one could make one "culture of music" one's own without sacrificing or compromising the other, was the utopia that both Webern as composer and Halm as apologist for Bruckner pursued. (Speaking of a utopia should be permitted insofar as the classicizing form that conjured up the spirit of the Beethovenian sonata seemed forced upon the dodecaphonic works of the twenties, and harmony, in Schoenberg's words, was "not under discussion at the time.") The formula "Bach and Beethoven," which epitomized for Schumann the legacy of a great past, appears as a cipher for an open problem that, because it imposed itself as irrefutably as it finally proved insoluble, belonged to the forces driving the development of music—absolute music—in the nineteenth and early twentieth centuries.

9

The Idea of the Musically Absolute and the Practice of Program Music

The battle over program music was waged from the eighteenth to the twentieth centuries with changing arguments resting on changing premises. And along with the esthetic theorems that apologias and polemics used to support themselves, the boundaries and defining characteristics of the thing itself changed as well. Program music is not a uniform phenomenon, but one that varies over history: not only in the trivial matter of style, the compositional means with which one attempts to paint, characterize, or narrate musically, but also (less obviously) esthetically, in the basic ideas that underlie the genre.

In the late eighteenth century, the "painting" genre—the attempt to imbue a piece of instrumental music with "content" by having it depict an aspect of external nature or represent a scene—was abandoned or at least repressed in the name of the esthetic postulate of sentiment: that music should move the heart. (Beethoven, who had mocked the tone painting in Haydn's *Creation*, justified "painting" in the *Pastorale*—which served the program musicians of the nineteenth century as a classic example—without denying it, by declaring that the "expression of sentiment" predominated.)

In contrast, romantic music esthetics, as mentioned above, distinguished the "programmatic" (musical story-telling), along with the "characteristic," from the "purely poetic," a category interpretable as esthetic idea of absolute music, but that may not simply be equated with the musically absolute as understood half a century later by Eduard Hanslick (however useful at first it may be to emphasize the affinity between Tieck's and Hanslick's theories in order to avoid the crude misunderstanding that the esthetic of the musically poetic aimed at a "literarization" of music). Without damaging or endangering the idea of absolute music, a music dissolved from functions, texts and characters while exalting itself to an "intimation of the infinite," there was certainly room for ambiences and even for suggestions of subjects in the realm of the musically poetic; for instance, in Mendelssohn's *Melusine* Overture, which Schumann reviewed in the spirit of romantic concepts of "poetry," musical representation did not exceed the "realm of wonder" in which E. T. A. Hoffmann had established absolute music, i.e., it did not lapse into the "prosaic," the opposite of the "poetic," through the pedantry of storytelling, characterization, or tone painting.

The dispute between the "New Germans" and the "formalists" over the legitimacy or illegitimacy of program music, which hardened into a partisan battle of musical politics around 1860, can be viewed as an attempt by each group to deny the other's right to the concept of the "spiritual in music." Whereas Franz Brendel, the ideologue of the New Germans, maintained that, by going from "indeterminate" expression of feeling to "determinate" characterization and programmatic content, modern instrumental music had progressed from the level of "sentiment" to that of "spirit," the Hanslickian esthetic of the "specifically musical" was based on just the opposite theory: that spirit in music was form, and form spirit. Musical form was not a mere manifestation that formed the shell or vessel for a content that, as idea, subject, or feeling, comprised the true essence of music; instead, as spiritual formation of sounding matter, it was itself "essence" or "idea." (In interpreting the concept of musical form, the Platonic-Neoplatonic dialectic of essence and manifestation was confused with the Aristotelian dialectic of matter and categorical formation.) But if, as Hanslick expressed it in a challenging paradox, "form moving in sound" is itself "content," then a programmatic content appears as an "extramusical" supplement to a form capable of existing for itself as "spirit in material competent to the spirit," instead of counting as a spiritual "essence" that has been referred to the musical "manifestation" so as not to remain vacuous.

In the late nineteenth and early twentieth centuries, the quarrel over the utility and disadvantages of program music (when it was not being continued using the arguments of Brendel and Hanslick) fell into a twilight area in that the ideas had lost their firm outlines. Almost all apologists for program music belonged to the followers of Wagner, whereas Wagner himself had appropriated the esthetic of Schopenhauer in 1854, which, to put it bluntly, was none other than an esthetic of absolute music.

Emotional stirrings, in which Schopenhauer believed he recognized the "true essence" of things, are expressed by music according to their "form" but "without substance," i.e., without object or motivation. But musically represented affections display their true essence without distortion precisely in their dissolution from the empirical conditions into which they are otherwise interwoven. "All possible endeavors, arousals, and expressions of the will, all those interior processes of man that reason relegates to the broad, negative concept of emotion, are expressed by the infinite number of possible melodies, but only in the generality of mere form, without the substance, always only according to the essence, not according to appearance, as though they were their innermost soul, devoid of a body."[1] Schopenhauer turned the standard, commonplace idea that in a piece of vocal music the text expresses the conceptually understandable "sense" of the whole, a sense that the music elaborates with "emotional reflections," into precisely its opposite, by claiming that the emotion depicted by music represents the actual "sense" of the work, whereas a poetic text or scenic process, when "underlaid" to a piece of music, remains thoroughly secondary. The conceptual or scenic part appears as the exterior, the emotion or affection as the interior. "This profound relationship that exists between music and the true essence of all things also explains the following: when one hears music that is appropriate to some scene, action, process, or setting, and it seems to reveal the innermost sense of the thing and appears as its most correct and clearest commentary; likewise, when one who gives himself over entirely to the effect of a symphony feels as though he were seeing all possible events of life and of the world pass before him—and yet, when he reflects, cannot describe any similarity between that music and the things that he had in mind." However, Schopenhauer considers the borders separating the associations that impose themselves on a hearing of instrumental music, the models of program music, and the texts of program music, to be indistinct, as all of them —relative to the essence of music—can be categorized negatively as incidental. "This is why one may set a poem as a song, or a visual representation as a pantomime, or set both to music in an opera. Such individual pictures of human life, set to the general language of music, never correspond or connect to it with complete necessity; rather, they stand in the same relation to it as an arbitrary example does to a general concept.[2] Schopenhauer does not distinguish in principle, but only in degree, between the process of "illustrating" music through a text or scenic action and the digressions of an imagination that lets a symphony stimulate it to visual images that transport it; in both cases, the impressions and concepts in which the central, musically expressed affect is reflected are secondary and, in principle, interchangeable.

One is involuntarily reminded of Eduard Hanslick, who likewise viewed literary or depictive programs as "extra-musical," esthetically "irrelevant" additions to instrumen-

tal music while denying the substantial unity and insepa-
rability of text and music in vocal music. The standard
reading of Hanslick, in which the attacks on program music
are taken seriously but the skeptical and malicious passages
on vocal music are dismissed as pranks and quirks, is
thoroughly inadequate and utterly unjustified. Instead, no
matter how uncomfortable the admission might be, a
historian should not deny that, in the rigorous esthetic of
absolute music, Schopenhauer's as well as Hanslick's, both
the texts of vocal music and the models of program music
were treated as "extramusical" incidentals, which are
interchangeable in principle and from which a musical
imagination that retreats to the essentials can abstract
itself. (The analogous, equally strict countertheory is found
in Franz Brendel's assertion that not only the text of vocal
music but also the model of program music belong to the
"thing itself," to the "esthetic object" the listener must
keep in mind in order to penetrate to the "meaning" of the
work as it is constituted in the interaction between subject
and sounding phenomenon.)

The most meaningful document of Wagner's reception of
Schopenhauer—next to the hesitant appropriation of
several fundamental ideas in the open letter "On Franz
Liszt's Symphonic Poems" of 1857—is the Beethoven
treatise Wagner wrote in 1870 for the centenary of
Beethoven's birth. (Nietzsche used it as the basis of his
panegyric to *Tristan* as absolute music.) Wagner's succinct
statement that his "dramas" were none other than "musical
acts made visible"[3] —denying the thesis of "Opera and
Drama" of 1851, that music was the medium and drama the
purpose of expression, in favor of the reverse, Schopenhauer's thesis that music expresses the essence that is
merely reflected in verbal and scenic appearance—is,
however, first expressed in the commentary "On the Term
'Musical Drama' " of 1872.

That Wagner, although he made Schopenhauer's metaphysics of music his own, sketched a text for Beethoven's

Quartet in C-sharp minor, Op. 131 that was intended to "present the image of a day in the life of our hero," must not be misconstrued either as a draft of a "program" or as biographical "reduction." It does seem at first as though the music were being biographically (or pseudobiographically) "decoded." "I should like to designate the long introductory Adagio, which must be the most melancholy statement ever made in tones, as the awakening on the morning of a day 'that, in its long course, will not fulfill a single wish, not one!' But it is simultaneously a penitential prayer, a consultation with God on faith in the eternal good."[4] What may, on cursory reading, appear as an "explanation" of the music on the basis of the external biography, is really the sketch of an "inner," "ideal" biography: "ideal" insofar as Wagner does not reconstruct Beethoven's life in order to decipher the music, but rather immerses himself in the meaning of the music in order to comprehend a piece of the "inner" biography that is inaccessible to empirical research. Wagner is convinced, using as his example the *Eroica* and its dedication to Napoleon, that just as there is little of substance to be learned about the meaning of a composer's works from his biography,[5] conversely, the "essence" that expresses itself in music—the substance of the empirical "appearances" such as one withdrawn into esthetic contemplation may develop—is highly revealing of the "inner" biography of the composer. But even the inner biography, the construction of an "ideal subject" of music, does not, according to Wagner, belong to the "thing itself." "Thus I have chosen the great C-sharp minor quartet, using it in order to express a true Beethovenian day in the life through its innermost processes. We would hardly succeed in this while listening to the work, for then we feel the need to let go immediately any specific comparison and only receive the immediate revelation from another world; but, to a certain degree, it is possible to do this if we merely consider this composition in our memory."[6] Wagner evidently did not

133

see that the musical phenomenon as it appears in an impartial hearing of a piece of instrumental music—at least a nineteenth century one—includes the experience of an "esthetic subject," as whose "expression" the music appears, and which is the subject not of the "external" but of the "internal" biography, the empirically and documentarily irredeemable correlate to esthetic experience.

Through Wagner's reception of Schopenhauer's esthetic, to which the composers of modern music felt bound, the theory of program music became complicated, sometimes to an extent that seems labyrinthine. The creation of works and their essence, empirical conditions and metaphysical meaning, biographical and esthetic forces all taken together make for a complicated configuration in the conceptual constructions with which one attempted to justify the practice of program music without surrendering Schopenhauerian principles. (The fact that Schopenhauer's metaphysics elevated the value of music to the immeasurable was doubtless a reason—along with their dependency on Wagner—why composers found it hard to divorce themselves from it.)

"Nothing (regarding its appearance in life, mind you) is less absolute than music."[7] "Thus we agree on this point and concede that divine music needed to be endowed in this human world with a binding, even—as we saw—determining force to make its appearance possible."[8] Enabling conditions of music, according to Wagner, include both speech and dance or scenic action: music, to appear, to realize itself, requires a "form motive," a raison d'être. But Wagner the Schopenhauerian distinguishes the metaphysical—or, as he says, the "divine"—essence of music from its "appearance in life."[9] That music is incapable of realizing itself without an extramusical "form motive," without taking shape in the composer's imagination, therefore in no way rules out the possibility of a listener's penetrating through the "appearance" and its conditions to the "essence," i.e., to perceiving the "will," which, according to Schopenhauer, makes up the substance of music. "Form motives," even though they belong to the conditions for the creation of music, are not its essential moment. Esthetic validity—the "essence," as it reveals itself in absent-minded esthetic and metaphysical contemplation—and actual, empirical genesis of the work go separate ways.

The consequences for the theory of program music were quite strange. To a disciple of Schopenhauer, programs—as influences on composition or reception: as "form motives" or as hermeneutic "parables"—are acceptable for the very reason that they do not touch the substance of the music, and thus do not matter. The apologia, even of the composers themselves, tends to an argument that is basically a plea for tolerance based on indifference. Under the rule of Schopenhauerian esthetics, programs—regardless of the function they claimed and of the emphasis with which they were presented—were considered too weak to be able to touch the "absolute" essence of music.

When Wagner, in the Beethoven treatise of 1870, attempted to justify the *Pastorale* in the spirit of Schopenhauer, he was using the Platonic thought pattern of traditional esthetics, the dialectic of essence and appearance. Hegel's statement that beauty is the "physical appearance of the idea" is still valid. But the idea that shines forth from the physical phenomenon is found to be, not nature, whose essence is revealed in the musical manifestation of the *Pastorale*, but quite the opposite: music, or musical form, which—as image of the "will"—makes the inner essence of natural phenomena perceptible. In using the classic example of the *Pastorale* to explain the esthetic character of program music, of the depiction of nature, Wagner is supporting himself, as did earlier theories, with the conceptual schema of "essence and appearance"; but nature and music have, so to speak, traded places in the dialectical relationship.

"And now the musician's eye was illuminated from

within. Now he cast his eye on the manifestation that, lit up
by his inner light, again communicates in wonderful
reflections with his inward self. Now, though, only the
essence of things speaks to him and shows him this" — the
manifestation — "in the calm light of beauty. Now he
understands the forest, the brook, the meadow, the blue
ether, the jolly crowd, the loving couple, the song of the
birds, the passage of the clouds, the rushing of the storm,
the joy of blissfully moved peace . . . 'Today you shall be
with me in Paradise' — who would not hear this word of
the Redeemer if he were to listen to the *Pastorale*
Symphony?"[10]

A heterogeneous set of things was lumped together in the
negative concept of the "extramusical" and therefore
"incidental." Within it, reasons and occasions for composing, hidden literary or pictorial subjects, programs that
claimed to be part of the "esthetic object," hermeneutic
decipherings, and coincidental associations, all flowed into
one another. In *The Birth of Tragedy*, Nietzsche denied
that there was a fundamental difference between interchangeable "depictions," i.e., those differing from listener
to listener (such interchangeability having already been
defended by the Beethoven enthusiast Wilhelm von Lenz
against the charge that it represented the bankruptcy of
poeticizing hermeneutics) on the one hand, and a program
intended and put into words by the composer on the other:
one "example" of a "general concept," to use Schopenhauer's term[11] was as "arbitrary" as another. But interchangeability, just as in the logical relation between the general
and the specific, in no way meant that metaphor was
esthetically vacuous. Although it exemplified instead of
determining, that did not make it superfluous or inadequate. "Here I call attention to a familiar phenomenon of
our own times, against which our aesthetic raises many
objections. Again and again we have occasion to observe
that a Beethoven symphony compels its individual auditors
to use figurative speech in describing it, no matter how

fantastically variegated and even contradictory may be the composition and make-up of the different worlds of images produced by a piece of music. To exercise one's poor wit on such compositions, and to overlook a phenomenon which is certainly worth explaining, are quite in keeping with this aesthetic. Indeed, even when the tone poet expresses his composition in images, when for instance he designates a certain symphony as the 'Pastorale' symphony, or a passage in it as the 'merry gathering of rustics,' these two are only symbolical representations of music—and not the imitated objects of music—representations that can teach us nothing whatsoever concerning the Dionysian content of music, and that indeed have no distinctive value of their own beside other images."[12] The generosity with which Nietzsche endows both secondary hermeneutics and primary programs stems from his opinion that they are irrelevant.

Among the premises of Schopenhauer's and Nietzsche's esthetic, the only argument against program music that could strike a nerve was the claim that a work needed an external literary crutch in order not to fall apart, because its inner musical coherence was brittle. (If, on the other hand, one starts from Franz Brendel's principles, i.e., from the premise that the program of a symphonic poem belongs to the work as an esthetic object, then this argument loses its substance: in this case, to put it trenchantly, it is just as irrelevant as the determination that a piece of vocal music remains incomprehensible without its text.)

Since Otto Klauwell had defined program music by saying that "renouncing the laws of the creation of musical form, it adapts the norms of its development to extramusical considerations wherever it goes,"[13] one can understand why Richard Strauss relinquished the term "program music": "So-called program music does not actually exist. It is an epithet in the mouths of all those who have no ideas of their own."[14] New forms such as an Otto Klauwell could not understand and whose artistic character he therefore denied, he blamed on the odious influence of "extramusical" circumstances. In contrast, Strauss insisted that it is narrowminded to dismiss unschematic works as "formless" instead of searching for the individual formal law, and that neither the existence or nonexistence of a program betrays anything at all about the inner musical logic of a work, or of its absence. "A poetical program may indeed suggest the creation of new forms; however, when music does not develop logically out of itself "—i.e., when the program is supposed to replace something—"it becomes 'literature music.' "[15] Thus it doesn't matter whether or not a program operated as an impulse: in worthwhile pieces, musical logic appears as a context that is closed within itself, and that neither needs nor tolerates an external crutch. If musical form (according to Schopenhauer or Nietzsche) is to be an "essential form" (with a program as its reflection in the world of appearances) and not a "manifested form" (with the programmatic content as its substance), then it must be based in itself. The "inner essence" of program music—which "doesn't exist"—is absolute music.

Gustav Mahler's letters of 1896 to Max Marschalk, in which he reflected on the meaning of the programs or title drafts for the First and Second Symphonies, are eloquent documents of the convolutions into which a theory of program music under the sign of Schopenhauerian esthetics was almost bound to fall. Mahler distinguishes between an "external" and an "internal" program. The external one can fulfill the function of an impulse during the conception of the work as well as that of a connecting thread for its reception. Referring to the First Symphony: "In the third movement (*Marcia Funèbre*), however, it turns out that I got the external idea through the familiar childrens' picture (*The Hunter's Funeral Procession*). But at this point, the thing to be depicted is irrelevant—only the mood that is supposed to be expressed is relevant."[16] "Therefore it is a good thing in any case, if for the time being, while my style still alienates them, the listeners are supplied with some" — programmatic — "signposts and milestones on their journey . . . But such a representation cannot offer more than that."[17] The "signposts" serve as a means of reaching an end, namely, an internal musical comprehension; and they fulfill their purpose in a merely preliminary way: "for the time being." If, however, it is true of the external program as a guide to reception that it does not approach the actual nature of the music (and Mahler says this unmistakably), then the same is obviously true of the external program as stimulus to composition: it is esthetically "irrelevant." Although it functions as a "form motive," as Wagner would say, it does not belong to the "thing itself," just like a scaffolding that one tears down as soon as the house it helped to build is finished. Thus it moves from a mediating function in the creation of the work to a heuristic one in its reception: in one sense it appears as a suspended force, in the other as a preliminary vehicle.

Whereas the "external" program presents itself as a sequence of images, the "internal" one is a "process of sensation,"[18] albeit one that is out of reach of empirical psychological categories. "My need to express myself musically, symphonically, only begins where the dark sensations rule, at the door that leads into the 'other world'; the world in which things are no longer separated by time and place."[19] But, according to Wagner (whose Beethoven treatise Mahler certainly knew), belonging "neither to time nor to space" is the inner nature of music as "harmony": only " by rhythmically ordering his tones does the musician thus come into contact with the visible, physical world."[20]

Mahler wrote of the Second Symphony: "I have called the first movement "Funeral," and, if you want to know, it is the hero of my D major Symphony whom I am bearing to his grave there, and whose life I, from a higher vantage point, collect in a clean mirror. At the same time, it is the great question: Why have you lived? Why have you suffered? Is it all just a great big, horrible joke?"[21] The "hero" is neither Jean Paul's "Titan," to whom the program of the First Symphony refers, nor Mahler himself, but rather, as Hermann Danuser recognized,[22] an "esthetic subject" of the music that, like the "narrator" of a novel or the lyric "I" in a poem, belongs to the esthetic stock of the work itself. If distortion of the esthetic experience is to be avoided, one must not identify with either the hero of the literary model or the actual person of the composer; the "external stimulus" through the former and the empirical substance of the latter are equally suspended by the musical form, which, according to Schopenhauer, represents the "inner essence of the world." The "internal" program is in no way to be sought in things comprehensible through biography or document, things that instead belong to the matter that was consumed by the musical form; instead it consists of a "process of sensation" made of feelings "in the abstract": "dark sensations." Thus the context that allows the idea of an "internal" program to make sense is the romantic metaphysics of instrumental music. Feelings dissolved from the empirical world form the substance through whose sacralization—in the esthetic of Wackenroder and Weisse—"absolute" music aspires to an intimation of the "absolute," and thus avoids the suspicion of being "empty form."

10

Absolute Music and *Poésie Absolue*

In his "Ideas Toward the Promotion of Musical Hermeneutics" of 1902, an attempt to create a theoretical
foundation for the exegetic practice of the "concert-hall
guide"[1] by reaching back to the doctrine of the affections of
the eighteenth century, Hermann Kretschmar wrote: "In
the sense of a merely musical content, there is no absolute
music! It is as much an absurdity as absolute poetry, i.e.,
a metered, rhyming poetry without ideas, would be."[2]
Whether Kretschmar was thinking of Stéphane Mallarmé's
poetry or intended to demonstrate the absurdity of the
principle of absolute music by conjuring up an analogy he
considered absurd and unreal (not knowing it had been
realized by the Symbolists) is not clear and need not be
determined. But it seems worthwhile to pursue the comparison he outlined, even if, unlike him, one is convinced of the
historical reality and the esthetic justification of both
absolute music and *poésie absolue*. (*Poésie absolue* is Paul
Valéry's term for Mallarmé's *Poésie pure*.)[3] Without
placing exaggerated hopes in a "mutual enlightenment of
the arts," as Oskar Walzel proclaimed half a century ago,
one may compare nineteenth century concepts of what is
essentially "poetic" to ideas of the same era regarding the
artistic character of music in order to discover relationships that do not exhaust themselves in mere wordplay.

But the attempt to spin ideohistorical threads between
romantic music esthetics and Symbolist poetry is burdened

with a methodological difficulty that can only be avoided if one retreats to the representation of a structural-historical coherence instead of claiming that there are connections in the form of historical events. Werner Vordtriede, in his book *Novalis and the French Symbolists*,[4] had little success in portraying the "astonishing similarity" between poetological tendencies of German Romanticism at the beginning of the century and French Symbolism at the end of the century as a real historical dependency, Carlyle's 1829 essay on Novalis being a weak, brittle connecting link; and it would be similarly futile to claim a documented connection between the principles of absolute music and *Poésie absolue*. The idea of absolute music (without the term) appears in E. T. A. Hoffmann, and, inversely, the term (without the idea) appears in Richard Wagner; but even though Hoffmann and Wagner were among the few influential Germans in the French culture of the nineteenth century, this fact does not even suffice to construct the hypothesis that the poetry of Baudelaire and Mallarmé was dependent on music-esthetic premises. And reference to the *Zeitgeist* that, without knowledge of the historical actors in the various arts, pervades them as a common substance would be grasping at a methodological straw from which nobody expects support anymore. (One cannot avoid hearing a reminiscence of the concept of "absolute music," which has become a commonplace in the twentieth century, in Valéry's term *poésie absolue*; but the belated coinage implies nothing about any music-esthetic implications of the original poetic idea that Mallarmé originally, from 1863 onward, called *poésie pure*— a term that has predominated until the present day.)

Although the similarity of the terms is therefore secondary, and a real-historical interdependency of the theorems hardly plausible, it can nonetheless be enlightening to discover the relationships between forms of esthetic thought in literature and to seek an explanation for the fact that the substance of artificial music was sought in the "poetic," and, inversely (after Walter Pater's famous dictum that all art constantly aspires to the condition of music), the nature of pure poetry was sought in the "musical" realm, even though actual works of literature were not meant in the former case, nor actual music in the latter. Above all, however, the sketch of structural connections between music esthetics and poetic theory is intended as support for the claim that the concept of absolute music—the esthetic paradigm that dominated the German concept of what music was in its essence from the heyday of the symphony and string quartet to the era of music drama—was a secular idea that represented the artistic feelings of an entire age.

1. In an essay on the "most recent development of international lyric," on "concrete, experimental, visual, phonetic poetry," Pierre Garnier—seeking historical anticipations or premonitions that would allow recognition of a tradition of modernism—quoted a Novalis fragment from the year 1798: "If one could only make it clear to people that it is the same way with language as with mathematical formulas. They make up a world of their own—they play only with themselves, express nothing but their wonderful nature, and for just that reason are they so expressive—for just that reason they mirror the strange play of the relationships between things."[5] At the same time, in *Fantasies on Art* (which appeared in 1799), Tieck was praising the musical tone system as "an isolated world for itself."[6] And the theory of language outlined by Novalis resembles—down to specifics of formulation and cadence—one of Tieck's dithyrambs to the symphony, in which music, independent of text and function, comes to itself. "But in instrumental music"—as opposed to vocal music—"art is independent and free, it alone prescribes its own laws, it fantasizes playfully and without purpose, and yet it fulfills and attains the highest purpose, it follows its dark urges completely and expresses the deepest, the most wonderful, with its triflings."[7] In early German romanti-

cism, the dream of absolute poetry was dreamed alongside that of absolute music. Rejection of the principle of imitation—the claim that music must represent either a piece of external nature through tone painting or a piece of inner nature through representation of affections, in order to avoid being empty sound, signifying nothing—went in parallel with the poetological insight that in lyric poetry as "true" poetry the language was the substance and not a mere vehicle of thoughts or feelings; that literature (as Mallarmé said, reacting in a spirit of ill- humor to the painter and literary dabbler Degas) is made of words and not of ideas.

Novalis says of poetic language nothing but that which romantic music esthetics claimed for instrumental music: precisely because it forms an "isolated world for itself " it is a metaphor for the universe, a tool of metaphysics. By making itself "absolute," tearing itself away from empirical conditions, it becomes an expression of the "absolute." However, the proposition that the theory of instrumental music had been the model for the theory of language would doubtless be an exaggeration that distorted an alternating effect into a one-sided dependency. (Seeking priorities, one might even claim that the esthetic-metaphysical doctrine— that autonomous art represents a metaphor of nature as a whole precisely because of its "dissolvedness"—was developed by Karl Philip Moritz between 1785 and 1788, primarily from the example of the visual arts.) The same fundamental idea, whose dialectic is contained in the double meaning of the word "absolute," reveals itself in various forms, in which the general, common tendency, specific preconditions of the specific arts, and mutual influences all interact with one another.

Werner Vordtriede recalls a Novalis fragment that has always been quoted as early evidence for a modern theory of poetry in the emphatic sense ever since the Symbolists discovered German romanticism in 1891. "Tales without coherence, yet with associations, like dreams. Poems, merely euphonious and full of beautiful words, yet also devoid of all sense and coherence—at most individual verses are comprehensible—like many fragments of the most diverse kinds of things. True poetry can at most have an allegorical sense in the large scale, and produce an indirect effect, like music, etc." Vordtriede comments: "Novalis did not create such formations of words. His ideas were far ahead of his practical poetry."[8] But the prose poems in which Wackenroder and Tieck, in *Fantasies on Art*, attempted to represent the effects of absolute music,[9] can certainly be understood as early realizations of the poetological agenda that Novalis designed: they are at the same time, and in the same sense, "tales without coherence" and "poems full of beautiful words, yet also without all sense and coherence," at most with "an allegorical sense in the large scale." And conversely, the Novalis fragment assembles a catalogue of the criteria that would make a description of music "purely poetic" in the romantic sense: it must proceed neither in a "programmatic" nor in a "characterizing" way, reaching instead for halting words in order to say the ineffable despite everything, namely by "saying" nothing according to the norms of everyday speech. Wackenroder's prose poems, reflections of what one extracted from hearing absolute music, are as patched together, associative, dreamlike, and allegorical as Novalis demanded. "Pure poetry," the ideal that romanticism had in mind (and which Schiller mistrusted as enthusiasm), appears as the means of expressing or indicating the "purely poetic" nature of absolute music.

One need hardly mention that poetry has always had individual verses that made their impression more because of their sounding nature than by actually saying something comprehensible or perceptible. What happened in romanticism, first in theory, but also, through Brentano, in poetic practice, was new merely in degree and not in principle. But the shift of emphasis was still sufficient to deeply change the awareness of what poetry was in the first place.

(One could, in a dialectic manner, speak of a change from quantity to quality.) The "musical" force of poetry was no longer considered ornamental and accidental; now it was seen as substance and nature.

Conversely (as was shown in an earlier chapter), instrumental music's claim to being taken seriously as a manifestation of "pure art," rather than being dismissed as empty sound, was nourished by literary models that guided a new musical consciousness to its formulation, through which it was able to constitute itself as musical consciousness in the first place. The metaphysical prestige of absolute music came about via a transfer of the poetic idea of unspeakability, a transfer whose locus classicus is the passage about the Stamitz concerto in Jean Paul's *Hesperus*. The allegro, the main movement of the symphony, which had previously been denigrated as being mere sound, received esthetic respect in the late eighteenth century by being received in the spirit of Klopstockian ode writing and Klopstock's "neobaroque" poetics. Where Sulzer had still seen it as "not unpleasant" but empty noise, Johann Abraham Peter Schulz—in Sulzer's *General Theory of the Fine Arts*—praised it as "sublime." What had been below language was now ennobled as being above language.

Therefore, it is in no way pointless or superfluous to inquire about those parts of the romantic idea of absolute art that truly belong either to poetic theory or to music esthetics, despite the interactions that should be emphasized. Whereas the theme of unspeakability, one of the fundamental premises of the artreligion, was of literary origin, it would seem as though the recourse to mathematics through which Novalis expressed his idea of "purely poetic language" has its esthetic-historical home in music theory instead of poetic theory: Pythagoreanism, even in its appropriation and transformation by romanticism, is primarily music esthetics. But it is especially meaningful that, although there existed high-quality instrumental music around 1800 to which an esthetic of absolute music could attach itself (albeit by reinterpreting the original esthetic purpose of the classical symphony), the theory of absolute poetry at that time was mainly a playful anticipation whose experimental and groping realizations manifested themselves as verbal paraphrases of the "purely poetic" nature of absolute music. One may marvel at the boldness with which the idea of a *poésie absolue* was sketched seventy years before Mallarmé, as if in a vacuum, but one should not forget that it was music, classical instrumental music, that gave a theory of absolute art concrete historical substance.

2. In both poetic theory and music esthetics, the idea that language, like music, was "an isolated world for itself" became combined with a tendency to withdraw from the expression of sentiment, i.e., from the element in which the bourgeois public of the eighteenth century (insofar as it did not actually demand the edifying and didactic) had sought the nature of art. Friedrich Schlegel, who believed he had discovered an affinity between pure instrumental music and philosophical meditation, combined his insight that musical form was a thought process with a polemic against the "flat viewpoint of so-called naturalness"; the viewpoint from which music appeared as a "mere language of sentiment."[10] And in poetic theory, it was Edgar Allan Poe who firmly distinguished "the pure elevation" to be attained through poetry from "the excitement of the heart" that must remain excluded.[11] (Poe's "The Philosophy of Composition" represents to a certain extent the charter of *poésie pure*, and historical influence on Baudelaire and Mallarmé can be traced back to Poe, not to Novalis.) But the juxtaposition of "excitement" and "elevation" (just like August Schlegel's demand for "pure" esthetic effect freed from the "material soil" of everyday perceptions) reminds one of the contrast between the esthetic of sentiment in *Empfindsamkeit* and the romantic metaphysics of instrumental music. The esoteric music esthetics of the late eighteenth century, which distinguished the sublime atmosphere that a sym-

phonic allegro (like a Pindaric ode) generates from the mere touching of the heart that a simple song endeavors to achieve, supported itself, as mentioned above, on Klopstock's poetic theory, but it also seems to have affected the poetics of the nineteenth century in return. (To speak of a dependency, though, would be an exaggeration; it suffices that the idea of an absolute music divorced from purposes and affections, yet not empty for that reason, but instead sublime, belonged to the "background knowledge" through which the adherents of a *poésie pure* found reinforcement.)

Absolute poetry, like absolute music, is esoteric: it appears as a thing of the avant-garde that, so to speak, is always fleeing the banal that it sees surrounding itself. And as the attacks on sentimentalism, beginning with those of Novalis and Schlegel, show, the sentimental was considered to be the most vulnerable to trivialization. (The fear of decaying into kitsch, which plagued the esthetic conscience of the avant-garde, is however not simply the other side of the esoteric coin, but seems to mean that kitsch, the mechanization of emotion, constituted the decadent form of an ideal still secretly sought after, despite all doctrines of *l'art pour l'art*: the ideal of original simplicity. It was the step from simplicity to the mechanical, from undisguised expression of the self to sentimentality put on for show, that was feared: a step that constitutes one of the small, all-important differences.)

3. The tendency of the poets of *poésie pure* toward the esoteric, toward rejecting the *profanum vulgus*, is related to a disgust with language that is threadbare and "besmirched" because everybody uses it every day. In music, one believed to have discovered a "pure matter" such as one dreamed of having for poetry. In an essay of 1862, "Art for All," Mallarmé polemicized against the "vulgarization of art": art must remain a mystery. And he complained that the hieroglyphic character that music possessed through its notation was lacking in poetry, which everyone considered accessible.

148

One hardly need mention that the idea of "pure musical matter" is an illusion based on a violent abstraction from the historical and social character of music: musical turns of phrase are no less exposed to wear and trivialization through commonplace use than are verbal ones. (What has happened to Debussy, an "esoteric" in Mallarmé's sense, is unspeakable: film music, in imitating his "tone," has neutralized it into a cliché that now colors the original works as well.) However, the very fact that the idea of "pure musical matter," however fictive, could come into existence and take on historical force, is based on a set of preconditions in the history of ideas that had their focus in the idea of absolute music. A quick sketch of these should not be superfluous.

In the music-esthetic tradition associated with the name of Jean-Philippe Rameau in the eighteenth century, one sought the origin of music (which simultaneously meant its nature) in "harmony," in "natural sound," whereas the opposing party, represented by Jean-Jacques Rousseau, saw music (meaning, for the most part, melody) as an imitation and stylization of human speech fulfilled by affections. But Rameau's faction associated the musical urphenomenon, the major triad contained in the series of partials, not man-made but a gift of nature, with vague concepts of musical mathematics and sounding hieroglyphics: concepts that might be represented by Bach's *Well-Tempered Clavier*, which progresses from evocation of the natural sound in the first prelude to contrapuntal depth in the fugue. In other words, one transported oneself through music into a sphere detached from both commonplace experience (which poetry also tried to escape) and the trivial thoughts to which "material soil" seemed to cling. Recourse to the natural sound justified above all an esthetic of instrumental music as "pure, absolute music" (albeit not in Rameau, but only in the romantic era): a contrast to Rousseau's derivation of music from passionate speech, a deduction that resulted primarily in an esthetic of vocal music. From 1800 on, the complex of ideas in which the concepts of natural sound, "pure matter," the use of instruments, mathematical calculus, and a *l'art-pour-l'art* distancing from feelings and affections were all blended together was the idea of absolute music. (The esthetic, art-religious demand for "pure," nature-given, non-man-made musical material was so overpowering in the nineteenth century that music theory never departed from the idea that modern tonal harmony was founded in natural sound, even though there were several objections so obvious that it took strong internal resistance to keep them from erupting into consciousness: for one thing, the overtone series could just as "naturally" produce musically unusable things as it could the major triad; also, it permitted a derivation from physics for chordal structure, but not for the all-important relationships between chords.)

4. From the same ideohistorical root as the desire for a "pure matter" in language and music comes the conception that a poet, by being nothing but a "literary engineer," evokes the "wondrous." Yet the quid pro quo of mechanism and magic, from craft and metaphysical meaning, which was just as characteristic of E. T. A. Hoffmann and Edgar Allan Poe as it was later on for Mallarmé and Valéry, seems to derive from the romantic music esthetic of the late eighteenth century, whence it transferred to poetics in Hoffmann. (One could undoubtedly spin the thread of the history of this idea all the way back to Pythagoreanism, but the feeling of dichotomy and contradiction is missing in earlier stages.) This is one of Wackenroder's central poetic-philosophical motifs; in his "Joseph Berglinger," the discrepancy between the "miracle of music" and the means of invoking it determines the "inner form" of the novella. In one of the fictional hero Berglinger's essays, which reflect the themes of the story, we read: "From what magic potion does the fragrance of this shining apparition arise? I look, and find nothing but a miserable web of numerical proportions, tangibly represented on bored wood, on racks

of gut strings and brass wires."[12] (The enthusiasm for the mathematical side of music that we find in Novalis seems dampened here; this is partly explained by the structure of the novella, partly by Wackenroder's taste for *Empfindsamkeit*.) Later, in an essay entitled "The Characteristic Inner Nature of Music, and the Spiritual Message of Today's Instrumental Music," Wackenroder writes: "Accordingly, no other art form has a basic material that is of itself already as pregnant with a heavenly spirit as music . . . some pieces are assembled by their composers like numbers in a calculation, or like lines in a schematic drawing: done merely correctly, but sensibly and at a fortunate time; and yet, when they are performed on instruments, they speak a glorious, expressive poetry — even if the master hardly imagined that, through his erudite work, the genius magically instilled in the realm of tones would beat its wings so marvelously for those souls who can perceive it."[13] It would undoubtedly be selling Wackenroder short to find in this passage nothing but the idea that knowledge of the formula is sufficient to conjure up musical "poetry" — a poetry that the composer need not know anything about, and that only reveals itself to the enthusiastic listener. The problem he was circling around, which is more easily recognized in the structure of the Berglinger novella than in the esthetic credos, consisted of the precarious dialectic between a mechanics that includes the spirit of music within itself and (except at a "fortunate time") imprisons it through pedantry, and an enthusiasm that understands the marvel of music but whose lack of craftsmanship keeps it from being productive — except at a "fortunate time." Mediation of the opposites is seen as an exception requiring a kairos; failure due to one-sidedness is the rule, and lends the novella its tragic aspect. However, in the esthetic of *poésie pure* (whose earliest document is the forced sobriety, the striking of a pose of literary engineering in Poe's "The Philosophy of Composition"), enthusiasm, the one side of Wackenroder's dialectic, was sacrificed, and the relationship between the constructiveness from which art emanates and the magic that is its result was emphasized all the more firmly and challengingly. And the metaphysics to which the romantic article of faith, that the construction of something poetic was a discovery of being, finally shriveled, was Mallarmé's metaphysics of nothing.

5. "The price of being an artist," said Nietzsche in *The Will to Power*, including himself, "is that one perceives what all non-artists call 'form' as the 'thing itself.' " This famous, challenging statement is practically a quotation of Hanslick's no less famous and challenging thesis, that "forms activated by sounding" are "uniquely and alone the content and object of music." And this thesis undoubtedly expresses a fundamental esthetic experience of nineteenth century "modernism": the experience that form in art, rather than being a mere manifestation of a thought or a feeling, is a thought in itself. A dictum of Paul Valéry (as reported by Valéry Larbaud) reads: "One would have to be a blockhead not to see that the proper or composed shape of a phrase, and thus of a verse, is an idea—just as important, just as general, just as profound as an idea in the ordinary sense."[14]

The esthetic of form that comprehended a musical or poetic form as essential form, as an intellectual or spiritual process manifesting itself in the material, rather than dismissing it as mere manifestation of content, was first and most forcefully formulated in the theory of instrumental music, because absolute music could only esthetically justify its existence in form. Instrumental music, lacking in object and function, and only partially comprehensible as a mere "language of feelings," required a legitimizing doctrine so as not to appear as pleasant but empty noise; this doctrine rested on the idea of essential form, on the "energeia" of "the spirit manifesting itself from the inside out."[15] True, the idea of "inner form" entered the consciousness of the nineteenth century through Wilhelm von Humboldt's philosophy of language (assuming one does without recourse to ancient philosophy, from which Shaftesbury took up the category in the eighteenth century); and, not coincidentally, Hanslick looked to Jakob Grimm, who shared essential premises of language with Humboldt, in order to support his idea that musical form was spirit and spirit in music was form. On the other hand, one should not deny that in the philosophy of music (above all through Nietzsche, who furnished Hanslick's sober doctrine with emphasis) the idea gained a pathos through which it was able to influence poetic theory in its own terms—and, as the example of Valéry (who had undoubtedly read Nietzsche) demonstrates, more effectively than in its original form in the philosophy of language.

There were two different explanations existing side by side in music esthetics and poetic theory for the thought that artistic form was essential form and not merely the form of a manifestation, that it needed to be construed as "spirit manifesting itself from the inside out" and not an "outer shell." Put formulaically, it means either that the content consists of the form, or that the form produces the content. If the content consists of the form, then, as with Hanslick, the determination of form as content means nothing other than that the spirit, which earlier esthetics had sought in the content, was to be found in the form. Hanslick dissected what was called content—the spirit together with the subject—reclaiming the spirit for the form, and sacrificing the subject. However, if, as in Edgar Allan Poe's poetics, the verbal form (which begins as a vaguely impending "tone" that takes shape in sound material and, through the material, attracts sharply delineated words and, eventually, thoughts) produces the content, then the traditional concept of the poetic process is transformed into its exact opposite. " 'Form,' the seeming result, is the source of the poem; 'sense,' the presumed origin, is the result."[16]

6. "The supreme object in the world, and the justification of its existence . . . could be nothing but a book."[17] Valéry's dictum, in which the metaphysics of art reaches an extreme, is the expression of that which Mallarmé thought and sought. The conceit that the substance of the world is destined to be absorbed in the book of the poet, a secularized appropriation of the metaphor of the world as a book, was the exalted presumption on which the theory of *poésie pure* was borne. On the other hand, Valéry's formulation, though not Mallarmé's thought, was unmistakably influenced by Nietzsche's dictum that "the existence of the world is justified only as an esthetic phenomenon."[18] And when Nietzsche, in the same context, spoke of art as the "true metaphysical activity of man," he meant music: the art of Richard Wagner interpreted in the spirit of Schopenhauer's philosophy.

But the dependencies, which we can reconstruct but vaguely, are not decisive; while the correspondences, which lie open before us, are. After all, the fact that the tendency to withdraw to pure forms was infused with a metaphysical justification in both poetry and music in the same epoch is ultimately far more strange and conspicuous than the mere translation of an esthetic theorem from one realm to the other would have been.

That art can be a process of abstraction consisting of the progressive dissolution of its contents was also recognized by Hegel, in his theory of instrumental music, in fact. And that the gradual departure from the positive and substantial, the retreat into the internal and formal, represents a necessary phase of intellectual history, which, in the final analysis, is the history of religion, is likewise a Hegelian thesis. But Hegel, who did not want to give up the priority of the firmly delineated word over formless intimation, would have been alienated by the consequence of his thesis: that art attains metaphysical dignity by its very retreat into the "empty inwardness" that Hegel identified as the arena of absolute music, of music that had come to itself. The paradox, that withdrawal means elevation, is the dialectic at the root of both *poésie absolue* and absolute music.

Notes

Chapter 1

1. Hanns Eisler, "Musik und Politik," in *Schriften 1924–1948.* (Leipzig, 1973), p. 222.

2. Jules Combarieu, "L'influence de la musique allemande sur la musique française," in *Jahrbuch der Musikbibliothek Peters, 2* (1895): 21–32, quoted (disapprovingly) in Arnold Schering, "Kritik des romantischen Musikbegriffs," in *Vom musikalischen Kunstwerk*, 2d ed. (Leipzig, 1951), p. 104.

3. Johann George Sulzer, *Allgemeine Theorie der schönen Künste* (Leipzig, 1793; reprint, Hildesheim, 1967), 3: 431–32.

4. Georg August Griesinger, *Biographische Notizen über Joseph Haydn* (Leipzig, 1810; reprint, Leipzig, 1979), p. 117.

5. Karl Philip Moritz, *Schriften zur Ästhetik und Poetik*, ed. Hans-Joachim Schrimpf (Tübingen, 1962), p. 3.

6. Horace believes the work of art should delight and edify (*Ars Poetica*, line 333).—*Trans.*

7. Moritz, *Schriften*, p. 4.

8. Ibid., p. 5.

9. Johann Mattheson, *Der Vollkommene Capellmeister* (Hamburg, 1739; reprint, Kassel, 1954), p. 82.

10. Ibid., p. 208.

11. In this paragraph, "sentiment" refers to "Empfindsamkeit," a German enlightenment esthetic current of the mid-eighteenth century. Corresponding to this was the musical "empfindsamer Stil," a vocal and instrumental style so designated by contemporary writers.—*Trans.*

12. Sulzer, *Allgemeine Theorie*, pp. 478f.

13. Wilhelm Heinrich Wackenroder, *Werke und Briefe* [ed. Friedrich von der Leyen] (Berlin, 1938; reprint, Heidelberg, 1967), p. 245.

14. Klaus Kropfinger, "Der musikalische Strukturbegriff bei E. T. A. Hoffmann," in *Bericht über den internationalen musikwissenschaftlichen Kongress Bonn 1970* (Kassel, 1973), p. 480.

15. E. T. A. Hoffmann, *Schriften zur Musik*, ed. Friedrich Schnapp (Munich, 1964), p. 34.

16. Arnold Schering, *Vom Musikalischen Kunstwerk* (Leipzig, 1951), p. 90.

17. Wackenroder, *Werke und Briefe*, pp. 218f.

18. Ibid., pp. 249f. Tieck contributed this and two other essays to the collection of Wackenroder's essays he edited after his friend's death.—*Trans.*

19. Hoffmann, *Schriften zur Musik*, p. 37.

20. Christian Friederich Daniel Schubart, *Leben und Gesinnungen* (Stuttgart, 1791; reprint Leipzig, 1980), 1: 210–11.

21. Gustav Schilling, *Encyklopädie der gesammten musikalischen Wissenschaften* (Stuttgart, 1838; reprint, Hildesheim, 1974), 6: 547.

22. Paul Bekker, *Die Sinfonie von Beethoven bis Mahler* (Berlin, 1918), p. 12.

23. Heinrich Christoph Koch, *Musikalisches Lexikon* (Frankfurt, 1802; reprint, Hildesheim, 1964), p. 1386.

24. "Triest," "Bemerkungen über die Ausbildung der Tonkunst in Deutschland im achzehnten Jahrhundert," *Allgemeine Musikalische Zeitung*, 3 (1801): 297–308.

25. Hoffmann, *Schriften zur Musik*, p. 19.

26. Ibid., p. 24.

27. Wackenroder, *Werke und Briefe*, pp. 226 and 255.

28. Christian Gottfried Körner, "Über Charakterdarstellung in der musik," in *Ästhetische Ansichten* (Leipzig, 1808), pp. 67–118; reprinted in Wolfgang Seifert, *Christian Gottfried Körner, ein Musikästhetiker der deutschen Klassik* (Regensburg, 1960), pp. 147–58.

29. Ibid., p. 4.

30. Hoffmann, *Schriften zur Musik*, p. 37.

31. Schilling, *Encyklopädie*, p. 348.

32. Adolf Bernhard Marx, *Ludwig van Beethoven*, 4th ed. (Berlin, 1884), 1: 271.

33. Ibid, p. 275.

34. Ibid., p. 274. Cf. also Marx, *Die Musik des neunzehnten Jahrhunderts und ihre Pflege*, 2d ed. (Leipzig, 1873), p. 52.

35. Friedrich Theodor Vischer, *Ästhetik oder Wissenschaft des Schönen*, 2d ed. (Munich, 1923), 5:381.

36. Robert Schumann, *Gesammelte Schriften über Musik und Musiker*, ed. Martin Kreisig (Leipzig, 1914), p. 338.

37. Carl Maria von Weber, *Sämtliche Schriften*, ed. Georg Kaiser (Berlin, 1908), p. 337.

38. Ibid., p. 339.

39. Ferdinand Hand, *Ästhetik der Tonkunst* (Jena, 1841), 2:405.

40. Ibid., p. 386.

41. Vischer, *Ästhetik*, pp. 338f.

42. Friedrich Nietzsche, "Über Musik und Wort," in *Sprache, Dichtung, Musik*, ed. Jakob Knaus (Tübingen, 1973), p. 25.

Chapter 2

1. Richard Wagner, *Gesammelte Schriften und Dichtungen*, ed. Wolfgang Golther (Berlin and Leipzig, n.d.), 2:61.

2. Ibid.

3. Ibid. 3:55.

4. Ibid. 2:56.

5. Ibid. 3:80.

6. Klaus Kropfinger, *Wagner und Beethoven* (Regensburg, 1974), p. 136.

7. Ludwig Feuerbach, *Grundsätze der Philosophie der Zukunft*, critical ed. Gerhard Schmidt (Frankfurt am Main, 1967).

8. Ludwig Feuerbach, *Kleine Schriften*, ed. Karl Löwith (Frankfurt am Main, 1966), pp. 81, 216ff.

9. Wagner, *Gesammelte Schriften* 3:255.

10. Ibid. 3:89.

11. Ibid., pp. 100f.

12. Kropfinger, *Wagner und Beethoven*, pp. 139f.

13. Wagner, *Gesammelte Schriften* 3:278f.

14. Ibid., p. 83.

15. Ibid., 86.

16. Ibid., p. 83.

17. Ibid., p. 84.

18. Ibid.

19. Ibid., p. 85f.

20. Ibid., p. 278.

21. Ibid., 5:191f.

22. Eduard Hanslick, *Vom Musikalisch-Schönen*. (Leipzig, 1854; reprint, Darmstadt, 1965), p. 20. [There are two English translations of this work, though neither is based on the first edition (see below, note 23). They are: *The Beautiful in Music*, tr. Gustav Cohen (London and New York, 1891; reprint, New York, 1974); and *On the Musically Beautiful: A Contribution towards the Revision of the Aesthetics of Music*, trans. and ed. Geoffrey Payzant (Indianapolis, 1986). Cohen translated the seventh edition, Payzant the eighth. Payzant's translation is much closer to the text and philosophical undercurrents in the original.—*Trans.*]

23. Hanslick, *Vom Musikalisch-Schönen*, p. 104.

24. Robert Zimmerman, "Vom Musikalisch-Schönen," in *Österreichische Blätter für Literatur und Kunst* (1854); quoted in Felix Gatz, *Musik-Ästhetik in ihren Hauptrichtungen*, (Stuttgart, 1929), p. 429.

25. Hanslick, *Vom Musikalisch-Schönen*, p. 32.

26. Karl Philip Moritz, *Schriften zur Ästhetik und Poetik*, ed. Hans-Joachim Schrimpf (Tübingen, 1962), p. 73.

27. Hanslick, *Vom Musikalisch-Schönen*, p. 34.

28. Friedrich Nietzsche, "Über Musik und Wort," in *Sprache, Dichtung, Musik*, ed. Jakob Knaus (Tübingen, 1973), p. 26.

29. Wagner, *Gesammelte Schriften* 3:231.

30. Nietzsche, "Über Musik and Wort," p. 28.

31. Ibid., p. 20.

32. Wagner, *Gesammelte Schriften* 9:111.

33. Nietzsche, "Über Musik und Wort," p. 30.

34. Friedrich Nietzsche, *Werke in drei Bänden*, ed. Karl Schlechta (Munich, 1954–56; Darmstadt, 1966), 2:1041.

35. Ibid., p. 914.

36. Arthur Schopenhauer, *Die Welt als Wille und Vorstellung*, Vol. I, section 52; in *Sämtliche Werke*, ed. Max Köhler (Berlin, n.d.), 2:258f.

37. Schopenhauer, *Sämtliche Werke* 2:261.

38. Nietzsche, *Werke*, 1:117.

39. Nietzsche, *Werke*, 1:116.

40. Nietzsche, "Über Musik und Wort," pp. 20f. Similarly, in the later "Human, All Too Human": " 'Absolute music' is one of two things: either form of itself, when music exists in the raw primitive

condition where sounding in measure and varying intensity gives pleasure all by itself; or the symbolism of the forms that, lacking any poetic text, speaks directly to the mind once the two art forms have been combined in a long period of development at the end of which music form is fully shot through with threads of concept and feeling" (Nietzsche, *Werke* 1:573).

41. Wagner, *Gesammelte Schriften* 9:77.

42. Ibid., p. 306.

43. Carl Friedrich Glasenapp, *Das Leben Richard Wagners* (Leipzig, 1911), 6:137f.

44. Ottokar Hostinsky, *Das Musikalisch-Schöne und das Gesammtkunstwerk vom Standpunkte der formalen Ästhetik* (Leipzig, 1877).

45. Hostinsky, *Das Musikalisch-Schöne*, p. 141.

46. Ibid., p. 145.

47. Ibid., p. 124.

48. Hermann Kretzschmar, *Gesammelte Aufsätze über Musik* (Leipzig, 1911), 2:175.

49. See Chapter 10.—*Trans.*

50. E.g., Rudolf Louis, *Die deutsche Musik der Neuzeit* (Munich, 1912), p. 156.

51. Ferruccio Busoni, "Sketch of a New Esthetic of Music," trans. Theodore Baker in *Three Classics in the Aesthetic of Music*, (New York: 1962), p. 78.

52. Ibid.

53. Ibid., p. 79.

54. Arnold Schoenberg, "Brahms the Progressive," in *Style and Idea*, ed. Leonard Stein (London, 1975), pp. 414f.

55. August Halm, *Von zwei Kulturen der Musik*, 3d ed. (Stuttgart, 1947), p. 39.

56. Ibid., p. 48.

57. August Halm, *Die Symphonie Anton Bruckners*, 2d ed. (Munich, 1923), p. 11.

58. Ibid., p. 12.

59. Ibid., p. 29.

60. Ibid., pp. 19, 46.

61. Ibid., p. 246.

62. Ibid., p. 240.

63. Ernst Kurth, *Bruckner* (Berlin, 1925), 1:258.

64. Ibid., p. 262.

65. Ibid., p. 264.

66. Ibid.

Chapter 3

1. E. T. A. Hoffmann, *Schriften zur Musik*, ed. Friedrich Schnapp (Munich, 1963), p. 34.

2. Ibid., p. 212.

3. Ibid., p. 36.

4. Ibid., p. 145.

5. Ibid., p. 215.

6. Ibid., p. 230.

7. Ibid.

8. Jean-Jacques Rousseau, *Dictionnaire de Musique* (Paris, 1768; reprint, Hildesheim, 1969), p. 242.

9. Ibid.

10. Ibid., p. 310.

11. Ibid., p. 306.

12. Johann Adam Hiller, "Von der Nachahmung der Natur in der Musik," in Friedrich Wilhelm Marpurg, *Historisch-kritische Beyträge zur Aufnahme der Musik*. Vol. 1, 1754–55. p. 542.

13. Johann George Sulzer, *Allgemeine Theorie der Schönen Künste* (Leipzig, 1794; reprint, Hildesheim, 1967), 4:478f.

14. Triest (pseud.), "Bemerkungen über die Ausbildung der Tonkunst in Deutschland," in Allgemeine Musikalische Zeitung (Leipzig, 1801).

15. August Wilhelm Schlegel, *Die Kunstlehre*, ed. Edgar Lohner (Stuttgart, 1963), p. 207.

16. Ibid., pp. 205f.

17. Ibid., p. 206.

18. Hans Robert Jauss, "Schlegels und Schillers Replik auf die 'Querelle des Anciens et des Modernes,'" in *Literaturgeschichte als Provokation* (Frankfurt am Main, 1970), p. 77.

19. Schlegel, *Die Kunstlehre*, p. 207.

20. Ibid., p. 221.

21. Ibid., p. 207.

22. Friedrich von Hardenberg (Novalis), *Fragmente*, ed. Ernst Kamnitzer (Dresden, 1929) pp. 524f., 578.

23. Jean Paul, *Vorschule der Ästhetik*, ed. Norbert Miller (Munich, 1963), pp. 93f.

24. Friedrich Wilhelm Joseph von Schelling. *Philosphie der Kunst* (Darmstadt, 1959), p. 144.

Chapter 4

1. *Hamlet* probably refers to incidental music to Shakespeare's play, written in 1779 by Georg Joseph Vogler (the Abbé Vogler). *Hamlet* captured the German imagination around that time, and remained popular into Wackenroder and Tieck's time. *Axur* is Lorenzo da Ponte's Italian version of Antonio Salieri's best-known opera, *Tarare*, originally to a French text by Beaumarchais. Both the original French version and the translation were extremely popular for thirty years following the premiere in 1787.—*Trans.*

2. Wilhelm Heinrich Wackenroder, *Werke und Briefe* [ed. Friedrich von der Leyen] (Berlin, 1938; reprint, Heidelberg, 1967), pp. 292f.

3. Ibid., p. 297.

4. Johann George Sulzer, *Allgemeine Theorie der schönen Künste*, 2d ed. (Leipzig, 1793; reprint, Hildesheim, 1967), 4:478.

5. E. T. A. Hoffmann, *Schriften zur Musik*, ed. Friedrich Schnapp (Munich, 1963), p. 34.

6. Wackenroder, *Werke und Briefe*, p. 255.

7. Hoffmann, *Schriften zur Musik*, p. 37.

8. Ibid., p. 34.

9. Karl Philipp Moritz, *Andreas Hartknopf* (Reprint, Stuttgart, 1968), p. 131.

10. Ibid., p. 132.

11. Ibid., p. 132ff.

12. Wackenroder, *Werke und Briefe*, p. 247.

13. Sulzer, *Allgemeine Theorie*, p. 479.

14. Jean Paul [Richter], *Werke*, ed. Norbert Miller (Munich, 1960), 1:775.

15. Ibid., p. 776.

16. Norbert Miller, "Musik als Sprache," in *Beiträge zur musikalischen Hermeneutik*, ed. Carl Dahlhaus (Regensburg, 1975), pp.271ff.

17. Gustav Becking, "Zur musikalischen Romantik", in *Deutsche*

Vierteljahrsschrift für Literaturwissenschaft und Geistesgeschichte (1924), 2:585.

18. Ibid., p. 586.

19. Wackenroder, *Werke und Briefe*, p. 256.

20. Ibid., p. 254.

21. Heinrich Besseler, "Mozart und die deutsche Klassik" in *Bericht über den internationalen musikwissenschaftlichen Kongress Wien 1956* (Graz, 1958), p. 47.

22. In Wolfgang Seifert, *Christian Gottfried Körner: Ein Musikästhetiker der deutschen Klassik* (Regensburg, 1960), p. 147.

23. Ibid., p. 148.

24. Wackenroder, *Werke und Briefe*, p. 255.

25. Ibid., p. 254.

26. Hoffmann, *Schriften zur Musik*, pp. 34f.

27. Hans Georg Nägeli, *Vorlesungen über Musik mit Berücksichtigung der Dilettanten* (Stuttgart and Tübingen), 1826, p. 32.

28. Ibid., p. 33.

29. Wackenroder, *Werke und Briefe*, p. 236.

30. Ibid., p. 255.

31. Friedrich von Hardenberg (Novalis), *Fragmente*, ed. Ernst Kamnitzer (Dresden, 1929), p. 586.

32. Friedrich Schlegel, "Charakteristiken und Kritiken *I*" in *Kritische Friedrich-Schlegel-Ausgabe*, ed. Hans Eichner (Munich, 1967), 2:254.

33. Abbé Dubos, *Réflexions critiques sur la Poésie et sur la Peinture* (Paris, 1715; reprint 1967); German trans. (Copenhagen, 1760), p. 413.

34. Eduard Hanslick, *Vom Musikalisch-Schönen* (Leipzig, 1854; reprint, Darmstadt, 1965), pp. 10ff.

35. August Wilhelm Schlegel, *Die Kunstlehre*, ed. Edgar Lohner (Stuttgart, 1963), p. 215.

36. Arthur Schopenhauer, *Sämtliche Werke*, ed. Max Köhler (Berlin, n.d.), 2:258f.

37. Hanslick, *Vom Musikalisch-Schönen*, p. 16.

38. Schopenhauer, *Sämtliche Werke*, 2:259.

39. Wackenroder, *Werke und Briefe*, pp. 222f.

40. Ibid., p. 206.

41. Ibid., p. 206ff.

42. Karl Wilhelm Ferdinand Solger, *Vorlesungen über Ästhetik*, ed. Karl Wilhelm Ludwig Heyse (Darmstadt, 1969), p. 340.

43. Ibid., p. 341.

44. To Weisse, like Schopenhauer, the "specifics" that an affection, in being a "beautiful affection," leaves behind mean the empirical, finite conditions, objects, and motivations of feelings.

45. Four years before Weisse, in his "Lectures on Music" of 1826, Nägeli had already spoken of a "hovering" in "the whole immeasurable realm of feelings" that means, in equal measure, both the suspension and the transfiguration of the affections. *Vorlesungen über Musik*, p. 33.

46. Christian Hermann Weisse, *System der Ästhetik als Wissenschaft von der Idee der Schönheit* (1830; reprint, Hildesheim, 1966), 2:56f.

47. Wackenroder, *Werke und Briefe*, p. 206.

Chapter 5

1. Johann Nikolaus Forkel, *Über Johann Sebastian Bachs Leben, Kunst und Kunstwerke* (Leipzig, 1802) ed. Walther Vetter (Kassel, 1970), p. 12.

2. Johann Gottfried Herder, *Werke*, ed. Heinrich Düntzer (Berlin, n. d.), 15:337.

3. Ibid., p. 341.

4. Ibid., p. 345.

5. Ibid., p. 350.

6. Ibid., 18:604.

7. Wilhelm Heinrich Wackenroder, *Werke und Briefe* [ed. Friedrich von der Leyen. (Berlin, 1938; reprint, Heidelberg, 1967), p. 245.

8. Herder, *Werke* 18:604.

9. Wackenroder, *Werke und Briefe*, p.115f.

10. Ibid., pp. 210f.

11. Ibid., p. 221.

12. Ibid., p. 251.

13. Ibid., p. 211.

14. Ibid., p. 254.

15. Ibid., pp. 226f.

16. Ibid., pp. 236f.

17. Ibid., p. 255.

18. Ibid., p. 283f.

19. Friedrich Schleiermacher, *Reden über die Religion*, ed. Hans Joachim Rothert (Hamburg, 1958), p.29.

20. Ibid., p. 30.

21. Ibid., p. 41.

22. Ibid., pp. 38f.

23. Friedrich Schleiermacher, *Glaubenslehre*, sec. 15; after Karl Barth, *Die protestantische Theologie im 19. Jahrhundert* (Hamburg, 1975), 2:385.

24. Ibid.

25. Hubert Schrade, *Deutsche Maler der Romantik* (Köln, 1967), p.17.

26. Johann Michael Sailer, *Sämmtliche Werke*. ed. Joseph Widmer (Sulzbach, 1839), 14:161f.

27. Ibid., p. 164.

28. Ibid., p. 166.

29. Ibid., p. 170.

Chapter 6

1. Friedrich Schleiermacher, *Reden über die Religion*, ed. Hans Joachim Rothert (Hamburg, 1958), pp. 92f.

2. Ibid., p. 93.

3. Wilhelm Heinrich Wackenroder, *Werke und Briefe* [ed. Friedrich von der Leyen] (Berlin, 1938; reprint, Heidelberg, 1967), p.251.

4. Ibid., p. 250.

5. Ibid., p.204.

6. Ibid., p. 211.

7. literally: love for, or adoration of, Jesus. Pietistic poetry often used the forms and metaphors of love poetry to express the idea of the personal relationship of the soul to Christ. —*Trans*.

8. Wackenroder, *Werke und Briefe*, p.120.

9. Ibid., p. 229.

10. Ibid., p. 230.

11. Ibid., p. 136.

12. Richard Alewyn, "Wackenroders Anteil," in *Germanic Review* 29 (1944):48ff.

13. Grell and Haller were the leaders of the Caecilian movement, which attempted to rescue the music of the Catholic church from a perceived decadence. Bruckner's motets reflect their influence to some degree.—*Trans*.

14. E. T. A. Hoffmann, *Schriften zur Musik*, ed. Friedrich Schnapp (Munich, 1963), pp. 229f.

15. Ibid., p. 232.

16. Ibid., p. 36.

17. Ibid., p. 235.

18. Ibid., p. 232.

19. Georg Wilhelm Friedrich Hegel, *The Philosophy of Fine Art*, trans. with notes, by F. P. B. Osmaston (London, 1920; reprint, New York, 1975), I:107. "Mind" is Osmaston's translation of "Geist" in this context. "Geist" also means "spirit," as in "Weltgeist," translated here as "world spirit."—*Trans*.

20. Ibid., p. 400, revised.

21. Ibid., p. 353–54, revised.

22. Ibid., p. 357, revised.

23. Ibid., p. 342, revised.

24. Ibid., 348–49, revised.

25. Christian Hermann Weisse, *System der Ästhetik als Wissenschaft von der Idee der Schönheit* (1830; reprint, Hildesheim, 1966), 2:49f.

26. Ibid., p. 51.

27. Hoffmann, *Schriften zur Musik*, p. 35.

28. Weisse, *System der Ästhetik*, 2:49.

29. Ibid., p. 55.

30. Ibid., p. 57.

31. Ibid., p. 53.

Chapter 7

1. I.e., dependent on another art form.—*Trans*.

2. Johann Gottfried Herder, "Viertes kritisches Wäldchen," in *Werke*, ed. Heinrich Düntzer (Berlin, n.d.), 20:482.

3. Johann Nikolaus Forkel, *Allgemeine Geschichte der Musik* (Leipzig, 1788; reprint, Graz, 1967), 1:24.

4. Ibid., p. 26.

5. Wilhelm Heinrich Wackenroder, *Werke und Briefe* [ed. Friedrich von der Leyen] (Berlin, 1938; reprint, Heidelberg, 1967), p. 250.

6. Ibid., p. 248.

7. Friedrich Schlegel, "Charakteristiken und Kritiken I," in *Kritische Friedrich-Schlegel-Ausgabe* ed. Hans Eichner (Munich, 1967), 2:254.

8. Ibid.

9. Johann Mattheson, *Der Vollkommene Capellmeister* (Hamburg, 1739; reprint, Kassel, 1954), pp. 235f.

10. Eduard Hanslick, *Vom Musikalisch-Schönen*, (Leipzig, 1854; reprint, Darmstadt, 1965), p. 32.

11. Ibid., p. 34.

12. Ibid., p. 35.

13. Ibid., pp. 99f.

14. Ibid., p. 35.

15. Ibid., p. 87.

16. Wilhelm von Humboldt, "Über die Verschiedenheit des menschlichen Sprachbaues und ihren Einfluss auf die geistige Entwicklung des Menschengeschlechts," in *Werke*, ed. Andreas Flitner and Klaus Giel (Stuttgart, 1963), 3:419f.

17. Ibid., p. 418.

18. Søren Kierkegaard, *Either/Or; A Fragment of Life*, trans. David F. Swenson and Lillian Marvin Swenson (Garden City, 1959; reprint, Princeton, 1971), p. 53.

19. Ibid., p. 54.

20. Ibid., p. 56.

21. Ibid., p. 55.

22. Ibid., p. 56.

23. Ibid.

24. Ibid., p. 52.

25. Ibid., p. 57.

26. Theodor W. Adorno, "Fragment über Musik und Sprache," in *Quasi una Fantasia* (Frankfurt am Main, 1963), p. 11.

27. Ibid., p. 11f.

28. Ibid., p. 14.

29. Ibid., p. 16.

30. Ibid., p. 11.

Chapter 8

1. Hans von Bülow, *Ausgewählte Briefe*, ed. Marie von Bülow (Leipzig, 1919), p. 36.

2. Robert Schumann, *Gesammelte Schriften über Musik und Musiker*, ed. Heinrich Simon (Leipzig, n.d.), 1:36.

3. Ibid., 1:113 and 3:153.

4. Ibid., 1:50.

5. Ibid., p. 44.

6. Ibid., 2:136.

7. Ibid., p. 44.

8. Richard Wagner, *Gesammelte Schriften und Dichtungen*, ed. Wolfgang Golther (Berlin and Leipzig, n.d.), 10:47f.

9. Friedrich Nietzsche, *The Birth of Tragedy and The Case of Wagner*. trans. Walter Kaufmann (New York, 1967), p. 119.

10. Martin Geck, "Bach und Tristan—Musik aus dem Geist der Utopie," in *Bach-Interpretationen*, ed. Martin Geck (Göttingen, 1969), p. 191.

11. Wagner, *Gesammelte Schriften* 7:130.

12. Ibid., p. 127.

13. Eduard Hanslick, *Vom Musikalisch-Schönen* (Leipzig, 1854; Reprint, Darmstadt, 1965), p. 35.

14. Wagner, *Gesammelte Schriften* 3:276ff.

15. Ernst Bloch, *Geist der Utopie* (Berlin, 1923), p. 89.

16. August Halm, *Von zwei Kulturen der Musik*, 3d ed. (Stuttgart, 1947), p. 253.

17. Ibid., p. 32.

18. Ibid., pp. 207ff.

19. Ibid., p. 13.

20. Ibid., p. 17.

21. Ibid., p. 16.

22. August Halm, *Die Symphonie Anton Bruckners*, 2d ed. (Munich, 1923), pp. 218 f.

23. Anton Webern, *The Path to New Music*, trans. Leo Black (Bryn Mawr, 1963), p. 35.

Chapter 9

1. Arthur Schopenhauer, *Sämtliche Werke*, ed. Max Köhler (Berlin, n.d.), 2:259f. The word translated here as "essence" is Schopenhauer's "An-sich.'"

2. Ibid., p. 260.

3. Richard Wagner, *Gesammelte Schriften und Dichtungen*, ed. Wolfgang Golther (Berlin and Leipzig, n.d.), 9:306.

4. Wagner, p. 96.

5. Ibid., p. 64f.

6. Ibid., p. 96.

7. Ibid., 5:191.

8. Ibid., p. 192.

9. Ibid., 9:75ff.

10. Ibid., p. 92.

11. Schopenhauer, *Sämtliche Werke* 2:260.

12. Friedrich Nietzsche, *The Birth of Tragedy and The Case of Wagner*, trans. Walter Kaufmann (New York, 1967), p. 54.

13. Otto Klauwell, *Geschichte der Programmusik* (Leipzig, 1910), p. 77.

14. Richard Strauss, *Betrachtungen und Erinnerungen*, 2d ed. (Zürich, 1957), p. 211.

15. Ibid.

16. Gustav Mahler, *Briefe*, ed. Alma Mahler (Berlin, 1924), p. 185.

17. Ibid., p. 188.

18. Ibid., p. 185.

19. Ibid., p. 187.

20. Wagner, *Gesammelte Schriften* 9:76.

21. Mahler, *Briefe*, p. 189.

22. Hermann Danuser, "Zu den Programmen von Mahlers frühen Symphonien," in *Melos/Neue Zeitschrift für Musik* (1975), p. 15.

Chapter 10

1. These encyclopedic volumes of program notes have long been popular in German-speaking countries; except as opera guides, they have never found a similarly wide audience in the English-speaking world.—*Trans.*

2. Hermann Kretzschmar, *Gesammelte Aufsätze über Musik* (Leipzig, 1911), 2:175.

3. Paul Valéry, "Je disais quelquefois à Stéphane Mallarmé," in *Variété III* (Paris, 1936), p. 15; quoted by Ernst Howald, "Die absolute Dichtung im 19. Jahrhundert," in *Zur Lyrik-Diskussion*, ed. Reinhold Grimm (Darmstadt, 1966), p. 47.

4. Werner Vordtriede, *Novalis und die französischen Symbolisten* (Stuttgart, 1963), p. 41.

5. Friedrich von Hardenberg (Novalis), "Monolog," in *Schriften*, ed. Richard Samuel (Stuttgart, 1960), pp. 672–73; discussed by Pierre Garnier, "Jüngste Entwicklung der internationalen Lyrik," in *Zur Lyrik-Diskussion*, pp. 451f.

6. Wackenroder, *Werke und Briefe* [ed. Friedrich von der Leyen] (Berlin, 1938; reprint, Heidelberg, 1967), p. 245.

7. Ibid., p. 254.

8. Vordtriede, *Novalis*, p. 170.

9. Wackenroder, *Werke und Briefe*, p. 226f. and 236f.

10. Friedrich Schlegel, "Charakteristiken und Kritiken," in *Kritische Friedrich-Schlegel-Ausgabe*, ed. Hans Eichner (Munich, 1967), 2:254.

11. Edgar Allan Poe, "The Philosophy of Composition," in *Works of Edgar Allan Poe*, ed. E. C. Steadman and G. E. Woodberry (New York, 1895; reprint, Freeport, N.Y. 1971) 6:42. Cited in Howald, "Die absolute Dichtung," p. 62.

12. Wackenroder, *Werke und Briefe*, p. 205.

13. Ibid., p. 221.

14. Valéry Larbaud, *Paul Valéry* (Paris, 1931), p. 64; quoted in Howald, "Die Absolute Dichtung," p. 70.

15. Hanslick, *Vom Musikalisch-Schönen* (Leipzig, 1854; reprint, Darmstadt, 1965), p. 34.

16. Hugo Friedrich, *Die Struktur der modernen Lyrik* (Hamburg, 1956), p. 38.

17. "Le suprême objet du monde et la justification de son existence . . . ne pouvait être qu'un livre." Paul Valéry, "Lettre sur Mallarmé," in *Variété II* (Paris, 1931), p. 218; discussed in Howald, "Die absolute Dichtung," p. 70.

18. Friedrich Nietzsche, *The Birth of Tragedy and The Case of Wagner*, trans. Walter Kaufmann (New York, 1967), p. 22.

Index

Index

Index